Prai

A Comprehensive Gu

"Anyone that has read one of the several English translations of the famed *Bhagavad-gītā*, with its richness of life-affirming truth, may have come away feeling spiritually refreshed yet vaguely uncertain as to whether or not the *Gītā* upholds a clearly developed system of thought. With its sophisticated thematic approach, this *Comprehensive Guide* brings clarity to the *Gītā's* content in a most thorough and systematic way, inviting both first-time and seasoned readers to vigorously engage with the text while enjoying the rewards of deep understanding. Especially impressive is the fact that this volume not only provides the reader with a stimulating learning experience, but also serves as an exceptional reference book for specific topics. Thus, in terms of my own *Gītā* studies, I am happy to have the benefit of this *Comprehensive Guide,* as well as the excellent, highly literal, translation that comes with it. And I certainly will be recommending this book to my students of Indian philosophy."

– Kenneth Valpey Ph.D., Oxford Centre for Hindu Studies

"H.D. Goswami's Comprehensive Guide with Literal Translation provides readers with unique insight into the essential meaning of *Bhagavad-gītā*, with succinct, carefully crafted explications of complex philosophical themes. Concise yet thorough, this skillful exposition, containing hundreds upon hundreds of key *Gītā* references, affords a conceptual window into the core elements of Krishna's teachings to Arjuna. Throughout this work we are graced by the knowledge, Sanskrit expertise and personal illuminations of one who is not only a highly trained scholar, but also a widely experienced spiritual teacher. Goswami is thus to be commended for so eloquently polishing the various facets of this most precious and rare jewel of sacred literature so that we, the readers, may perceive that much more of its unbounded brilliance."

– Graham M. Schweig, Ph.D., Professor of Philosophy
and Religion, Christopher Newport University

"In the late 18th century *Bhagavad-gītā* became the first Sanskrit work to be rendered in a European tongue, and since that time it has generated countless translations and secondary analyses. Among these, however, H.D. Goswami's *Comprehensive Guide with Literal Translation* excels in its capacity to schematize and summarize the *Gītā*'s powerful appeal as a source of perennial wisdom. The literal translation's careful nuancing demonstrates the author's Sanskrit mastery and philosophical expertise while the Guide's focused precision and theological depth reflect the training of a Harvard doctorate as well as the spiritual insight of one dedicated to the *sannyāsa* (renounced) order. Thematically divided into twelve parts, each with multiple subsections that focus on major issues, the Guide's strongest features are its expert pinpointing of verses that pertain to each theological topic and its contextual analysis, articulated in succinct crisp prose that eschew both academic jargon and sectarian rhetoric. It is an excellent resource not only for those approaching the Gītā as a spiritual manual, but also for those seeking a more systematic and rigorous understanding of its philosophical content. I look forward to using this work in my Hinduism courses."

– Edwin Bryant, Professor of Hindu Religion
and Philosophy, Rutgers University.

A Comprehensive Guide to

Bhagavad-gītā

With Literal Translation

H.D. Goswami

Krishna West, Inc.
Gainesville, Florida

Published by

Krishna West, Inc.
1515 NW 7th Place
Gainesville, FL 32603
website: www.krishnawest.com

ISBN: 978-0-9862403-0-0
Library of Congress Control Number: 2014958503

Text design and formatting by Mayapriya dasi, Bookwrights.com
Cover design by Danesha dasa

Printed in India and the United States of America
Published simultaneously in the United States of America and Canada by Krishna West, Inc.

Distributed exclusively by Torchlight Publishing, Inc.

Readers interested in the subject matter of this book or wishing to correspond with the author are invited to write to: bookinfo@hdgoswami.com

Contents

Comprehensive Guide

Literal Translation

A Note To the Readers

This *Comprehensive Guide*, with its many hundreds of systematic references to *Bhagavad-gītā* verses, is an ideal companion to the *Literal Translation* contained herein. Readers can approach this book in a variety of rewarding ways. For example, one can begin by reading the *Guide* straight through, or toggle back and forth between the *Guide* and the translation, or first read the translation and then the *Guide*. Some will prefer reading the book from beginning to end, while others may enjoy browsing the topics at their pleasure. Regardless of how one chooses to approach this unique book, many wonders are here to be discovered.

It is also important to note that in translating the *Gītā* the author has chosen to keep ambiguities in Sanskrit ambiguous in English as well. The *Gītā* clearly contains an explicit central message, but it also at times contains mystic and mysterious language, dense and intense philosophy and unique ways of self-expression, all of which the author has tried to retain in the English. The purpose of this elaborate *Comprehensive Guide* is to unpack, disambiguate and explain the literal translation such that the clear central meaning shines through.

Please note that bracketed numbers in the *Guide* indicate a *Gītā* chapter and verse. Thus [2.26] indicates Chapter 2, Verse 26.

Comprehensive Guide to
Bhagavad-gītā

PART I
Introduction

The words *Bhagavad-gītā* literally mean *The Lord's Song*, and today a billion people around the world accept it as such. This elegant, ancient text addresses life's biggest issues: Who am I? What is the universe? How can I be happy? Where does it all come from? Where is it all going? Who are real teachers and how do we recognize them? The *Gītā*, as it is often called, excels in its calm, reasonable, satisfying responses to these perennial questions.

A brief Sanskrit work of seven hundred verses, *Bhagavad-gītā* forms part of the *Bhīṣma-parva*, the sixth book of *Mahā-bharata*, a vast sacred history. The *Gītā* shines as the spiritual beacon and summit of that far larger work, which for untold centuries has played a central cultural role in South Asia and beyond.

Originally, this comprehensive guide to the *Gītā*'s content was intended to be only a short introduction to my literal *Gītā* translation. But like Kṛṣṇa's fabled fish incarnation, which appeared in tiny form and then grew to vast proportions, what began as a mere introduction, grew by necessity to become a book in itself. Having read, studied and cherished the *Gītā* for decades at the feet of my teacher Śrīla Prabhupāda, I could not help but share the profound conceptual connections that make this Sanskrit text so magical. The *Gītā* is widely recognized as a work of spiritual and philosophical genius, and early on I fell in love with its Sanskrit text. My sincere wish here, through explication and translation, is to bring the general reader deep within that original Sanskrit. I hope you enjoy the journey.[1]

Historical Context

Bhagavad-gītā opens on a battlefield moments before justice and injustice (*dharma* and *a-dharma*), personified by Pāṇḍava and Kuru warriors, burst into war.[2] Kṛṣṇa drives the chariot of Arjuna, His close friend and cousin, who fights for right. But just as the battle is about to begin, Arjuna falls into confusion. Claiming compassion for cruel usurpers with whom he shares family bonds, he refuses to fight for justice. Arjuna recognizes this emotion as weakness [2.7],[3] yet it paralyzes him. He cannot act. After trying to defend his retreat with socio-moral arguments and pleas, Arjuna nearly collapses in anxiety, and here ends the *Gītā*'s first chapter.

In Chapter Two, Kṛṣṇa begins to revive, teach and enlighten Arjuna, insisting on moral, social and spiritual grounds that Arjuna should indeed fight. Some readers question the *spirituality* of Kṛṣṇa urging Arjuna to battle. To understand what is going on, we must turn to the *Gītā*'s historical setting within the epic *Mahā-bhārata*.

Imagine you awake one day to shocking news: usurpers have seized your government, suspended the constitution, driven out the legitimate rulers and violently imposed martial law. You pray that the legitimate government, the military and

---

[1] A note to my readers: italics are used throughout my *Gītā* translation to emphasize key words and phrases as well as to highlight English words that are jargon or symbolic in their Sanskrit original.

[2] The *Gītā*'s first chapter, arcane to most with its long lists of warrior names, is thrilling to one who knows all the *Mahā-bhārata* history that came before.

[3] Numbers in brackets indicate *Gītā* verse numbers; thus [2.7] indicates Chapter 2, Verse 7.

all loyal citizens will oppose the aggressors and restore the rule of law and tradition.

Mahā-bhārata teaches that a similar crisis erupted in India thousands of years ago. Kṛṣṇa, God, came to Earth to help His devotees—Arjuna, his brothers and others—to restore *dharma* (justice, Law, legitimate rule) on earth. Thus, in *Bhagavad-gītā*, Kṛṣṇa urges Arjuna to oppose the Kurus, led by Duryodhana, who unjustly usurped power. Kṛṣṇa states that He expressly comes to earth to restore *dharma* [4.7–8], and here we see Him in action.

Legitimate rulers expect their generals to defend the law. So Kṛṣṇa expected Arjuna to fight at Kuru-kṣetra rather than allow rule by fraud, coercion and usurpation.

The events of this sacred history occur on three levels: earthly, cosmic and spiritual:

1. Earthly: we briefly spoke of this above.
2. Cosmic: the teachings of *Bhagavad-gītā*, and the encompassing history of *Mahā-bhārata*, unfold within a personal, multi-layered cosmos of upper, middle and lower worlds. Justice and injustice (*dharma* and *a-dharma*) contend in higher worlds as they do on earth. On the Kuru-kṣetra battlefield, where Kṛṣṇa speaks *Bhagavad-gītā*, the Kurus, Pāṇḍavas and all other leading warriors fought as empowered incarnations of cosmic heroes and villains (*Devas* and *Asuras*). Earth had become a battleground for a cosmic struggle.
3. Spiritual: when Kṛṣṇa, God, descends to this world, He designs His deeds, such as speaking *Bhagavad-gītā*, to awaken sleeping souls to their eternal, blissful nature and ecstatic relationship with Him. The entire history that frames the *Gītā* is a planned spiritual drama wherein Kṛṣṇa saves the virtuous, removes the wicked and restores *dharma*, the sacred Law that sustains the universe [4.8].

The Origins of the *Gītā*

What has scholarship said about the origin of *Bhagavad-gītā*? About fifteen hundred years ago, the great mathematician-astronomer Arya-bhata[4] concluded from archeo-astronomical data in the *Mahā-bhārata* that the Kuru-kṣetra War, the setting of *Bhagavad-gītā*, took place approximately 5,100 years ago.

Some modern scholars, especially from the West, have resisted such antiquity, speculating that the *Gītā* was composed roughly between the fifth and second centuries BCE.[5] Such scholars also often doubt the historicity of most *Mahā-bhārata* events, whereas other scholars (East and West), and most Hindus, accept both their antiquity and historicity. Who is right?

Limited empirical evidence does not allow worldly scholarship to definitively affirm or deny such claims, and much less to speak authoritatively about Kṛṣṇa's divinity. Just as declaring an algebraic equation right or wrong is to make an algebraic claim, so also declaring a metaphysical statement right or

---

[4] In addition to helping found trigonometry, Arya-bhata [476–550 CE] wrote astronomy books (such as an *ephemeris*) that were considered authoritative for centuries by both European and Islamic scientists and mathematicians. India's first satellite as well as a lunar crater were named after him, as were a university and a scientific institute.

[5] These scholars invariably date the *Gītā* after the time of Buddha, whose birth is believed to be in the 6th century BCE. Their reason: the *Gītā* five times [2.72; 5.24,25,26; 6.15] uses the word *nirvāṇa*, a term often used by Gautama Buddha. Clearly we have three possibilities here: 1) Kṛṣṇa borrowed the term from Buddha; 2) Buddha borrowed the term from Kṛṣṇa; and, 3) Kṛṣṇa and Buddha independently used the same word. On a prominent academic forum that includes many of the world's leading Indologists, I recently asked whether there is definitive evidence for *possibility one*—i.e., that Kṛṣṇa borrowed the term *nirvāṇa* from Buddha. No one was able to supply any such evidence, and one senior scholar wrote: "I don't think we can rule out the possibility that the term is pre-Buddhist." This notwithstanding, most Western scholars continue to assume, write and teach that the *Gītā* must be later than Buddhism because it uses the term *nirvāṇa*. Oh well . . .

wrong is to make a metaphysical claim. And the ground rules of worldly scholarship do not smile upon metaphysical claims.

The conclusion is that despite the plethora of learned *best guesses*, worldly scholarship lacks sufficient evidence to prove the date and origin of *Bhagavad-gītā* beyond reasonable doubt. Other extraordinary claims, such as Kṛṣṇa's assertion that He originally spoke the *Gītā* to a sun deity [4.1], entail no internal contradiction or other logical absurdity, and thus must remain sacred claims, also beyond the power of worldly scholarship to mark right or wrong.

Scholars often wonder whether the *Gītā* formed part of the original *Mahā-bhārata* or was added later. Again, a lack of historiographic evidence precludes a definitive academic response. In the twentieth century, the world's most distinguished Sanskritists attempted to reconstruct the original *Mahā-bhārata* from dozens of surviving recensions. After a half-century of brilliant assiduous study, they admitted that it is beyond the powers of worldly scholarship to recreate, and thus conclusively identify, an original version of this text. Thus scholarship can hardly determine whether the *Gītā* is part of an original text that no one can clearly reconstruct.

Scholarly controversies often burn hottest precisely where evidence is weakest and leaves the largest space for conflicting opinions. Questions of the *Gītā*'s original date and formation provide ample opportunity for just this sort of endless academic debate—which I intend to avoid here.

What we do know beyond doubt is that the *Bhagavad-gītā* has inspired and illumined a huge and growing number of souls. Kṛṣṇa's devotees claim that we have the very *Gītā* that Lord Kṛṣṇa intended for us. In their view, rather than battling over the *Gītā*'s provenance, we should take advantage of its profound wisdom, which has long lightened loads, gladdened hearts, excited intelligences and guided souls in their quest for ultimate meaning.

In *Bhagavad-gītā*, Kṛṣṇa teaches that there are three fundamental *real things*: souls, nature and God. He also teaches that God's relationship with fallen souls is mediated by the laws of *karma* and that awakened souls approach and relate to God through *yajña*, the process of devoted offerings. All this will be explained in the next five sections.

PART II
Individual Eternal Persons (*Puruṣa*)

The *Gītā* teaches that every living being in this world is an eternal soul encased in a temporary material body. Each soul has always existed and will always exist as a personal individual being [2.12]. Only the material body begins and ends [2.18], for the soul is never born and never dies [2.16–21]. The soul is God's superior living energy [7.5], a part of God, Kṛṣṇa [15.7]. And God is kindly disposed toward every soul [5.29].

Spiritual liberation entails neither giving up our individual existence nor merging into anything impersonal. Rather we shed layers of illusion and uncover our true self. Throughout *Bhagavad-gītā*, Kṛṣṇa refers to the soul as a *person* (*puruṣa*).[1]

An ever-changing material body covers the soul. The ancient Greek philosopher Heraclitus is reputed to have said that one cannot step twice into the same river, since its waters are constantly flowing. We might also say that one cannot breathe twice in the same body, since it is ever in biological flux. The body is the field on which we play out our life; we souls are the witnesses of that field [13.2].

Just as material objects exist in space but can never taint or transform it, so the body, though affecting our consciousness in many ways, can never alter the soul's eternal nature [13.33]. Simple reflection reveals that when we say "I was a child" or "I was an adolescent" or "I am an adult," the fundamental "I" (the core self) is the same constant person, even as body and mind change in so many ways [2.13]. That enduring "I" is the soul,

---

[1] 2.15, 2.21, 2.60, 3.4, 9.3; Arjuna: 13.1, 13.20–22, 13.24, 17.3.

and is not an illusion. Illusion occurs, rather, when we identify the "I" with a changing mortal body instead of with our true eternal self.

Completing our tenure in one body, we enter another, just as one gives up worn clothes and puts on new ones [2.23]. Only an excessively fashion-conscious person anguishes over the loss of a mere shirt or dress. So in illusion, we lose ourselves in grief over the inevitable change of body, forgetting that the body merely garbs an eternal soul.

The irony of mundane life is that for all our vanity, we drastically underestimate ourselves. We think ourselves mortal, when we are truly immortal. We endure painful limits to our knowledge and joy, yet as eternal parts of God, Kṛṣṇa, each one of us is entitled to innate and limitless awareness and joy. We need only claim them appropriately [6.20–22].

As we forget our eternal nature and cling to fleeting material objects, selfish desires drag us into illusion. Hundreds of "desire-chains" imprison souls who seek lordship of this world [16.12]. Even pious souls are bound by the mundane work born of their nature [14.6, 18.60].

Chasing the materially pleasant and fleeing the unpleasant, we fall into "duality-illusion," as desire and aversion overcome us [7.27]. Kṛṣṇa cautions us not to rejoice at the materially pleasant or grieve for the unpleasant [5.20]. Rather we should tolerate both, for both come and go, being mere products of sense perception [2.14].

Kṛṣṇa cites many examples of mundane dualities that arouse desire and aversion: cold and heat, joy and sorrow [2.14, 6.7, 12.18], gain and loss, victory and defeat [2.38], honor and dishonor [6.7, 12.19, 14.25], success and failure [2.48, 4.22, 18.26], love and hate[2] [2.64, 3.34, 18.23, 18.51], dirt, stone and gold [6.8, 14.24], friend

---

[2] Here love and hate indicate a passionate dualistic mentality in which one emotion feeds the other: we adore one person and neglect or denigrate

and foe [6.9, 12.18, 14.25], saints and sinners [6.9], weal and woe, lamenting and hankering [12.17], slander and praise [12.19, 14.24], the pleasing and displeasing [5.20, 14.24], thrill and misery [18.27]. For those entrapped in them, all these dualities are but other names for joy and sorrow [15.5].

Throughout the *Gītā*, Kṛṣṇa explains that even in this life, within our present body, we can rise to pure consciousness, know God and live in a state of spiritual liberation. At present, our material desires conceal our true awareness [3.39]. Thus, by our decision to embrace or reject spiritual life, we act as our own friend or enemy; we alone elevate or degrade ourselves [6.5–6]. Kṛṣṇa emphasizes that we are responsible for our own condition. The Lord does not force us to do good or evil, and thus is not responsible for the joy and sorrow we create in our lives [5.14–15]. We have *free will.*

Speaking on a historical battlefield that is also pregnant with symbolic meaning, Kṛṣṇa repeatedly tells Arjuna to conquer not only the military foes, but also illusion, the greedy senses and the impulsive mind. If we are to follow Arjuna and conquer the illusion that keeps each of us from enjoying the unlimited life we crave, we must learn more about material nature and exactly how it seduces and imprisons us through its modes or qualities.

---

others. Kṛṣṇa does not refer here to pure or spiritual love.

PART III
Nature's Three Modes (*Guṇa*)

Kṛṣṇa defines the primary material elements, physical and cognitive,[1] as His inferior nature [7.4]. As clothes cover the body, these temporary physical and cognitive elements cover the eternal soul [2.22], who is Kṛṣṇa's superior nature or energy [7.5].

All material objects, whether bodies or planets, are ever in flux [8.4], endlessly transforming into different forms and qualities. Yet material energy itself, the substance underlying nature's protean forms, is beginningless and permanent [13.20].[2]

Importantly, material nature manifests with primary perceptible qualities. The *Gītā* frequently uses the Sanskrit word *guṇa* to refer to nature's three basic qualities or modes: goodness, passion and darkness. Indeed, the entire fourteenth chapter focuses on these material modes.

As human color vision is trichromatic, based on three primary colors, so worldly life exists within a tri-modal system of goodness, passion and darkness. Just as we seldom find natural objects in pure primary colors, so the things of this world seldom embody pure primary modes. People and objects tend to show complex mixtures of the modes. Thus a person has a *good side*, but also a *passionate side*, and even a *dark side*. The material modes permeate every object, emotion, act and ambience in this world, including food, faith, work, worship, charity,

---

[1] The primary elements of nature are earth (solids), water (liquids), air (gases), fire (radiant elements), ether (space), mind (the seat of emotions and senses), reason (our analytic faculty), and ego (our full material identity).

[2] This notion of matter is somewhat analogous to Aristotle's *substance*.

philosophy, bodies and buildings. Indeed every free choice we make is a modal choice: good, passionate or dark—with infinite combinations.

Kṛṣṇa declares that nothing on earth or among gods in heaven is free of nature's modes [18.40]. How does this work in practice? Consider our attraction to other human bodies. Mere atoms or molecules do not send us swooning, for every physical body basically contains the same types of atoms and molecules. Rather when we see a body that exudes the modes that are *right* for us, we fall in lust. Conversely, opposing modes arouse our hatred. Thus bodies that are biologically the same but that exude different modes either bewitch or disgust a given observer.

Similarly, many houses are built of the same basic materials: wood, stone, cement, etc. But a house with a certain *style* or *feel*—i.e., a certain *mode*—either attracts, repels or leaves us unmoved, depending on the mode of consciousness we have cultivated in life.

In choosing friends, spouse, music, career, food, neighborhood, movies, recreation and everything else, we choose and attach ourselves to particular combinations of modes. Thus we either reinforce or transform the quality of our life.

For example, when we give charity for a good cause, solely to help others, and with no desire for return, we give charity in goodness [17.20]. When we help others, but also seek fame or profit through our gifts, we give in passion [17.21]. And giving that does more harm than good is in darkness [17.22], such as a gift that enables one with clear criminal intent to harm the innocent. Thus the quality or mode of our giving affects the quality of our life.

Kṛṣṇa gives a similar modal analysis of faith, food, sacrifice, austerity, renunciation, knowledge, action, the doer, reason, determination, happiness and vocation, explaining how each mode binds us, leading to varieties of future lives.[3]

Good, passionate and dark acts are all habit-forming. As we choose friends, places, music, food, work, etc. in various modes, we give those modes power over our lives [13.22]. Virtuous acts beget virtue; passion engenders passion; and dark behavior such as addiction, wanton violence, etc. traps one in darkness.

Our mode choices also shape our perception of reality. Thus consciousness in goodness perceives a deep spiritual unity within all differences of race, gender, species, etc. [13.31, 18.20], whereas passionate perception sees such differences as fundamental and final, with no ultimate unity [18.21]. Finally, cognition in darkness sees no truth at all in the world, and lacks any power of abstract thought [18.22].

Thus the modes are both moral and epistemic. That is, they reflect and condition the moral quality of our acts, and also govern how, and to what extent, we understand the world and ourselves. A passionate person may read piles of books, perform many experiments and contribute vastly to our material knowledge, but only the virtuous soul rises to the clear consciousness by which is seen the ultimate purpose and meaning of life.

Rising or falling in the universe, or staying where we are, depends on the mode we cultivate in life—the quality that motivates us and shapes our perception [14.8]. Nature's modes are not mere passive qualities, but rather active powers that force us to act [3.5]. Thus the passion mode gives rise to lust and anger, which compel us, even against our rational will, to act badly [3.36–37] or even wickedly [17.5].

---

[3] 17.2–4, faith; 17.8–10, food; 17.11–13, sacrifice; 17.17–19, austerity; 18.7–9, renunciation; 18.20–22, knowledge; 18.23–25, action; 18.26–28, the doer; 18.30–32, reason; 18.33–35, determination; 18.37–39, happiness; 4.13, 18.41–44, vocation; 14.5–8, bondage; 14.14–16, 18, our next life.

When we falsely see ourselves as ephemeral flesh, bodily cravings shroud our pure cognition [3.39], just as smoke covers fire, dust covers a mirror, or a womb covers an embryo [3.38]. Indeed lust, anger and greed are "gateways to darkness that ruin the soul" [16.21–22].

As we try to enjoy nature's modes, and cling to them, we take birth in good and bad wombs, based on the quality of our acts and choices [13.22]. By conditioning us to act materially, the modes bind us to this world [14.5]. Goodness, for example, fosters worldly joy and wisdom; but a good person clings to these [14.6] and thus cannot transcend *temporary* goodness to reach eternal life.

Our troubles begin when we *meditate* on a material sense object, attracted by its qualities. Attachment (*saṅga*) arises and the mind clings to that object, be it another person, a fancy car, a big house, a prestigious position, intellectual power or whatever. If we continue to contemplate that object, our clinging attachment turns into intense longing (*kāma*)—we lust for that object. When we do not achieve our wish or obtain the object of our lust, anger (*krodha*) arises; and even when we do, anger comes anyway, since no material object can satisfy the soul. In cases of intense desire, anger bewilders us and we forget what is truly important in life. Once we forget, we lose our reason and our real spiritual identity vanishes from our mind. Kṛṣṇa describes this entire sequence [2.62–63].

Saṅga, "attachment, clinging," is the mental glue that fastens us to objects embodying this or that mode. Thus we rotate through high and low bodies [13.22].

One might conclude that the mode-driven soul has no free will; but, in fact, the modes act upon us *only* when, and to the extent that, we try to exploit them. Consider this example: once we purchase a ticket, board a commercial flight and take off, we must accept the consequence of our act—we must fly to our destination. Yet even aboard the plane, we still have free will.

We may chat, sleep, watch a movie or even cause a disturbance that will lead to legal difficulties.

The Sanskrit word *vaśa* means "*control*," and the opposite, *a-vaśa*, means "without control, against one's desire or will." Repeatedly, Kṛṣṇa uses this word *a-vaśa* to show that our attempts to exploit nature cause us to fall helplessly under nature's control.[4] On the other hand, by spiritual practice one achieves real control over one's life.[5] Similarly, the law imprisons precisely that person who tries to live above the law. One who obeys just law, lives in freedom.

The modes bind us to this world, and in that bound state we cannot fix our mind on our eternal existence. Again and again we compulsively try to enjoy the world, regardless of what our pure reason, in the form of muffled, gagged conscience, tries to tell us about true self-interest. To transcend this illusory state, we must change our association. By associating with spiritual energy, spiritual people, etc., we revive our spiritual nature. We then easily, spontaneously, naturally act for our highest self-interest.

We do have free will, but we cannot avoid the consequences of our choices. The cosmic system that responds to our mode choices and delivers their consequences is called *karma*.

---

[4] 3.5, 3.34, 8.19, 9.8, 18.60.

[5] 2.61, 2.64, 5.13, 6.26, 6.36.

PART IV
Action, Reaction, Bondage (*Karma*)

Karma refers to the cosmic system that reacts to our free acts, delivering to us fair, commensurate consequences. In this way, the universe holds up a mirror to each soul.

The *Gītā* teaches that the universe consists of upper, middle and lower worlds [3.22, 11.20, 15.17], with Earth being a middle planet that Kṛṣṇa calls the *human world* [11.38, 15.2]. Life in all material worlds is temporary and unsatisfying for the eternal soul [8.15–16, 9.33]. Still, there are higher and lower levels of material life. By *karma's* laws, good acts raise us to higher states, passionate acts keep us where we are, and dark acts drive us down to lower states [14.18].

We experience these states (or reactions) in a series of lives. God never gives up on us. We have unlimited chances to discover the truth: that we are spiritual beings and our real home is Kṛṣṇa's eternal abode, not any place in this transient universe. We keep trying to enjoy and understand, birth after birth, till we achieve final liberation and return to our eternal home [6.45, 7.19]. (More about this final destination later.)

Yet endless opportunities in this world should not lull us into loitering here, since each new body entails the "flaw of birth, old age, disease and death" [13.9]. Indeed, Kṛṣṇa calls the karmic chain of rebirths *karma-bondage* [2.39, 3.9, 9.28], *the death-wandering-path* [9.3], *the death-wandering-ocean* [12.7] and *birth-bondage* [2.51], wherein one who is born must die and one who dies must again take birth [2.27]. Thus selfish acts, in which we cling to action's fruits, bind us to this world [5.12].

Under karmic laws, the soul in different bodies cycles through a universe that itself moves in endless cycles.[1] On earth, we observe cycles of days, nights and seasons, based on cyclical motions of earth, sun, moon and other celestial bodies. The *Gītā* teaches [8.16–19] that the entire universe, and the countless souls that populate it, move through grand cycles of cosmic creation and dissolution,[2] corresponding to days and nights of Brahmā, whom God (Kṛṣṇa) deputes to create the cosmos.[3]

After a hard day of work and study, one must replenish body and mind with restful sleep. Likewise, after eons of struggling and learning in the *karma* system, souls are given deep rest within Kṛṣṇa's own nature, only to be sent forth again [9.7] into this temporary world of suffering [8.15] till they learn to value spiritual freedom.

This description may strike the reader as rather gloomy. However, the *Gītā* offers a rich menu of paths that liberate us from the *karma* cycle of birth and death, and deliver us to our true, eternal life.

In fact, our *bondage* is essentially psychological. We impose upon ourselves a false, limiting identity—the mortal body—and then lament self-imposed limits. But just as we imprison ourselves in illusion, we can also free ourselves. No one else can free us if we do not free ourselves [6.5–7]. So why don't we make that choice?

Imagine a passenger in an airport transit lounge waiting to fly home. Distracted by items for sale, a new acquaintance

---

[1] Not only ancient Vedic and later Hindu culture, but many civilizations, such as the Incan, Mayan, Hopi, Babylonian, ancient Greek, Buddhist, Jain, etc., see time as cyclical.

[2] More elaborate texts, such as the *Purāṇas*, describe a type of cosmic reincarnation wherein multiple universes repeatedly, cyclically, take birth and die.

[3] Cf Plato's creator *demiurgous* (literally 'public worker') in the *Timaeus* dialogue.

or some annoyance, the passenger misses the flight. Similarly, oblivious to our eternal nature and ultimate happiness, we chase fleeting pleasures and flee from whatever displeases us, thus forgetting our real goal of life—our true destination. Desire and aversion overcome us and we fall into *duality-illusion* [7.27], wherein one side of duality dialectically brings its opposite.

Thus, if we gloat in victory, we will one day suffer in defeat; if we proudly rejoice at gain, we anguish over loss. Kṛṣṇa cautions us to neither rejoice at the materially pleasant nor lament the unpleasant, for both come and go, being mere products of sense perception [2.14].

Trapped in these dualities and their extremes of joy and sorrow [15.5], we love and hate material objects and forget that our real self exists beyond all material objects.

When we identify with the body, we cling to the fruit of the body's actions. We do this because we are locked into dualities of attachment and aversion and thus seek to enjoy what we like and avoid what we dislike. Since we thus lay claim to ownership of our actions, we are held responsible for the reactions to those actions as well. Simple! So we return to this world life after life to receive, enjoy and suffer the results of our actions—and that is *karma*.

Busy trying to enjoy this world, we imagine ourselves the center of reality and try to possess all that we desire in God's creation. Thus we fall into the illusion of "I and mine," egotism and possessiveness.[4] Ironically, a negative form of "I and mine" arises when we hate all that frustrates our selfish wishes.

This illusory psychology of duality, egotism and possessiveness keeps us helplessly wandering in the material world under the laws of *karma*. Yet by a simple technique we can instantly spiritualize our actions, transforming *karma-bondage* into *karma-yoga*, a path to spiritual liberation. Similarly, we

[4] 3.27, 16.18, 17.5, 18.24, 18.58, etc.

can transform our intellectual life, our pursuit of knowledge, into *jñāna-yoga* (knowledge-*yoga*), another path to spiritual freedom. What is that simple technique that spiritualizes every aspect of our life, from food to philosophy to work to love? It is *yajña*, the act of offering to God: deceptively simple, but powerful in practice.

PART V
Sacrifice or Offering (*Yajña*)

The very universe that binds us to *karma* offers us a path to freedom: *yajña*, offering. Apart from this loophole, or escape clause, the whole world is but an endless variety of *karma-bondage* [3.9]. One who makes no offering cannot enjoy this or any other world [4.31].

What then is *yajña*, offering? How does it play such an important role in cosmic function and personal salvation?

Kṛṣṇa teaches that we are created to offer sacrifice, for the creator builds it into our deep nature as creatures [3.10]. Virtually everyone offers something of symbolic or tangible value to a superior in order to please, placate, oblige or win favor. And whenever we do, we engage, in the most basic sense, in *yajña* (sacrifice). It is so much a part of our nature that even those who dismiss sacred texts and shun celestial rites perform *yajña* nonetheless. Thus people pay taxes (and bribes) to higher political powers. We ritually honor superiors in the military, at work, in government, on the athletic field, on campus, etc. People sacrifice time, energy, money, even their lives, for what they see as a *higher cause* or as a rational way to negotiate and navigate higher power. Thus *yajña* (offering) is a universal impulse, a need and an inspiration of people everywhere.

Not surprisingly, we find that virtually all religions engage the faithful in some sort of offering to divine or higher power, however conceived. Typically one seeks divine favor to secure safety, happiness, prosperity or enlightenment for oneself and one's dear ones, warding off evil and winning one's wishes. On rare occasions a devoted spiritualist seeks a divine being's pleasure as an end in itself, but that is not par for the human course.

Bhagavad-gītā carefully analyzes the offering act, making a crucial distinction between action (*karma*) and its fruit or reward (*karma-phala*). Driven by our nature, we must act at every moment [3.5], and our acts bear fruit: wealth, fame, power, knowledge, love or bodily pleasure. Remarkably, Kṛṣṇa tells us that we have a right *only* to our duty, but *never* to its fruits [2.47]. We must offer the fruits to those higher powers that bestowed them. Indeed *karma* binds us precisely when we grasp the fruit of work. Kṛṣṇa defines a selfish, binding act as one in which we cling to fruits [5.12]. If we reverse this motion, and first offer the fruit to its source before enjoying it, we perform *yajña* and free ourselves from *karma*.

One might well ask: "Why can't we enjoy the fruit of our own labor"? Actually we can, but only after first acknowledging our bounty's source. For example, offering our food before we eat does not mean that we *starve*; rather, by a simple rite of recognition, respect and gratitude, we free ourselves from the offense of taking without giving back [3.13].

Indeed the ability to feel gratitude and to reciprocate lifts us above abject savagery. By sincere offering, one escapes the blindest form of egotism. One escapes the tiny prison of self-centeredness, realizing that *something* or *someone* in the universe is greater than and provides for us.

But how does a primeval, innate, ubiquitous rite free one from *karma*? Is this merely a faith claim? Can anyone simply offer anything to any power, real or imagined, and get free from *karma*? Is it that easy? Not really. Just look at history: even murderous tyrants often made mystical or magical offerings [16.15, 17]. *They* certainly are not liberated souls.

Only a truly spiritual offering dissolves one's *karma* [4.23–24], but most people perform *yajña* as they perform all other acts: immersed in nature's modes [17.1–3, 17.11–13].

The *Gītā* presents a sweeping hierarchy of offerings, ranging from dark and demonic to divine and liberating. Let us review that hierarchy, for we will thus behold in clear colors the scale of consciousness—and of life itself.

Although Kṛṣṇa urges us to transcend this world by spiritual *yajña*, He also explains worldly *yajña* to help the reader become a good *comparison shopper*. Thus the *Gītā* presents the function, variety and limits of mundane offerings.

Chapter Three twice enjoins the worldly-minded to participate, through *yajña*, in a kind of cosmic economy that, properly tended, brings prosperity to all. In the first iteration of this duty, Kṛṣṇa simply states that people must make offerings to cosmic managers (*devas* or *gods*) who then supply all human needs [3.10–13]. With this bounty, humans then make further offerings that bring renewed bounty [3.14–15].

Thus *a cycle is made to turn* [3.16]: the cycle of receiving and giving back. If we do not keep this cycle turning, if we take but do not give back, then our heedless self-indulgence and ingratitude offend the natural order. We live in vain as thieves [3.12, 3.16]. On the other hand, if we eat after first offering we free ourselves from all sin [3.13].

Of course, most people today, though they accept the general principle of reciprocity, neither believe in nor offer to *gods*. Is Kṛṣṇa's talk of *gods* a bit of ancient myth mixed into an otherwise enlightening treatise? Should we sanitize such talk of *gods* with symbolic interpretations?

Before doing so let us consider who the gods really are in *Bhagavad-gītā*. Otherwise, for a modern reader, the term *gods* may conjure images of cartoonish ancient pantheons or pagan challenges to monotheism.

First, gods are not *God*. Second, they carry out rational duties: they manage a big corporation called *the universe*. Keep in mind that the modern West still uses divine language to name rich and powerful humans.[1] Third, these cosmic administrators are far superior to us; hence we cannot demand instant access to them any more than ordinary citizens can demand intimate meetings with the world's most powerful leaders.

But even if one chooses to suspend contemporary incredulity, one might still object to *yajña* on the grounds that God seems to be doing business instead of just loving us. Yet Kṛṣṇa enjoins offerings to gods only for *unmindful* souls who *do not* care about God but *do* try to enjoy His creation. Indeed, no sooner does Kṛṣṇa enjoin these offerings than He adds a caveat: one who delights in self alone, satisfied in self alone, need not offer to gods [3.17–18]. Only those who are intent on enjoying *this* world must pay a luxury tax on mundane pleasures. Those who find higher pleasure in soul and God, and do not try to exploit His creation, need not make such offerings. Yet Kṛṣṇa requests that they do so anyway, so as to set a good example for the unenlightened. He even cites His own example [3.20–26]. Indeed, when He came to this world, Kṛṣṇa performed many standard duties to teach others.

This is the real reason for *yajña*: those who seek to possess this world need to rise above the bestiality of seizing what they want with no regard for its ultimate source and proprietor. By offering back to God's agents, who rule the very world one seeks to enjoy, one awakens one's higher ethical nature. Thus the materialist escapes the tiny prison of self-centeredness and connects to a vast, just, personal cosmic community.

After all, civilization itself depends upon our capacity for justice, our willingness to respect each other and give others their due. *Karma* imprisons us precisely when we try to grasp and monopolize the fruits of our own work. Why? Because in

---

[1] Thus with German *Herr*, Italian *Signore*, Portuguese Senhor, Spanish *Señor*, French *Monsieur* and even English *Sir*, one politely addresses men with a word that either means or is derived from *Lord*. And in most of these cases, there is a precise feminine equivalent. So we have Sanskrit *deva*, god.

doing so, we violate a universal law of civilized beings: those who take should offer back, value for value. Only the delusionally wicked believe themselves to be independent, autonomous lords of the world [16.14]—though, as we shall see, even this select group makes a crazy kind of offering.

By sincere offering we learn, as science now confirms, that giving bestows more joy than taking, that generosity surpasses greed. The reciprocity that is the heart of *yajña* sustains justice in our minds, societies and civilizations. We realize that our bodies, our bounty and our lives—and the natural world that sustains all these—come as gifts from above. So the *Gītā* teaches.

At the same time, most of us are, as the saying goes, "works in progress." Many emotions besides pure love and gratitude fill our hearts. Thus regardless of their religion—be it animistic, polytheistic, monistic, monotheistic or secular humanist—people make mundane offerings as they do almost everything else: under the spell of nature's three modes. We will explore the variety of mundane offerings in the *Gītā*'s own general, non-sectarian terms.

Let us start at the material bottom and work our way up to final spiritual liberation. Holding the bottom rung is the wicked offering. History displays all too many villains whose atrocities caused cruel suffering to humanity and the rest of nature. In Chapter Sixteen Kṛṣṇa profiles the wicked: they claim there is no *Truth*, only truths, no God, only competing selfish pursuits [16.8]. These depraved individuals flourish by harming others, and put the world gravely at risk [16.9]. Mad with pride and presumption [16.10], they will kill anyone for their gain, for they claim to be lords of the world, "rich, mighty, perfect and happy" [16.13–14].

These are not the kind of people you want as neighbors. Yet these twisted figures, in mad pursuit of power, make offerings, as the *Gītā* states [16.15] and all history confirms. Kṛṣṇa calls these offerings *nāma-yajña*, "offerings in name only": "stubborn and vain, the wicked offer hypocritically with no care for rules" [16.17]. In the next verse Kṛṣṇa adds that such sacrificers "hate and envy God in their own and others' bodies" [16.18]. In other words, the wicked do not offer to please or honor a greater power. Rather, immersed in self-adoration, they seek greater power by ritually exploiting what they believe to be an amoral magical power source. The final goal in such *offerings* is to harass, enslave and terminate other people. Harry Potter would understand this problem!

Apart from demonic offerings, the *Gītā* describes *yajñas* that are more conventionally corrupted by nature's three modes. Here is the triad.

The offering in darkness resembles the wicked rite in that it is chaotic, faithless, without charity and tendered to strange spirits and ghosts [17.4, 13]. But this rite has no explicitly evil intent.

Passionate people tend to offer to guardian spirits and other supernatural benevolent beings. These rites display an urbane hypocrisy: one appears to give, but really seeks personal gain and fame [17.4, 12], though again, there is no explicitly evil intent.

Those dealing in dark and passionate *yajñas* have not even seriously accepted the cosmic managers, the *gods*. So there is no question, at this level, of a profound or devoted monotheism.

Those in goodness do offer to God's trusted agents, the gods, with sincere attention and without seeking any selfish return. They offer because they believe "it is the right thing to do," and they follow rules given in sacred texts [17.4, 11].

In one sense, true *yajña* begins here, in goodness. In darkness, one offers in confusion, hardly knowing what one does. Passionate *yajña* is more a shrewd investment than a devoted gift—one gives to get. In goodness, one at last has a sincere moral sense of offering to greater beings, of doing right for its own sake. Yet even in goodness, one offers to gods rather than God [17.4]. Thus one still lacks full awareness of *who* truly deserves one's gift [5.27, 9.24, 13.23] and *who* ultimately sends the reward [7.20–22].

A survey of Sanskrit words used in this context reveals how Kṛṣṇa wants us to relate to His agents, the gods: we should not take final shelter of them (*prapad*) [7.20], nor devote ourselves to them (*bhakti*) [9.23], nor swear our ultimate allegiance to them (*vrata*) [9.25], but we should *honor* them in the way that we honor priests, teachers or the wise (*pūjanam*) [17.14]. Indeed honoring gods is listed, along with cleanliness and honesty, as part of a decent disciplined life.

So what is the status of the *yajñas* described above? They all incur *karma*, for they all unfold within nature's modes, yielding quick but fleeting fruits [4.12, 7.23]. Thus those who seek success *in karma*, not freedom *from karma*, offer to gods [4.12]. Only by offering to God (not gods) in full knowledge can one be actually liberated [4.30]. Even if by worldly *yajña* one rises to this world's heaven, one will fall back again [9.20–21]. Advanced spiritual *yoga* takes one beyond the best rewards of worldly offerings [8.28], all of which are ultimately inappropriate [9.23] and do not lead to God, for they do not aim at God [7.23, 9.25]. They do not help us to see God [11.48]. Conclusion: be careful to whom you make your offering.

Nevertheless Kṛṣṇa teaches that even a mundane *yajña* is better than no *yajña* at all. Even if one has no wish to serve God, one must at least pay cosmic taxes on all the natural resources we receive from God's agents. However, there are greater things available than *good karma*. There is actual spiritual life, a key to which is the spiritual *yajña*, which we will now consider.

When we forget our Source, and thus our own true nature, we try to exploit this world. Illusion (*māyā*) then covers our real awareness [3.39] and we imagine that we are matter: the material body. However, when we devotedly offer our actions to the Supreme, we uncover real knowledge: that we are eternal parts of God [15.7]. Like fallen sparks placed back in fire, we then blaze with pure knowledge and joy.

As we have seen, the *Gītā* emphasizes that one should offer to God, not to gods. After all, we are eternally part of Kṛṣṇa [15.7]. Thus it is natural to serve God, as much as the hand naturally serves the body of which it is part. By feeding the body, the hand nourishes itself.

Kṛṣṇa refers to Himself as the Enjoyer[2] of offerings (*yajña*) [5.29], in fact the Enjoyer and Lord of all offerings [9.24]. Failing to recognize the categorical difference between God and gods, one falls from the spiritual plane [9.24]. *Bhagavad-gītā* thus teaches that only an offering to the Supreme Lord keeps one on the highest spiritual plane. Kṛṣṇa urges us, for our highest good, to offer to Him [9.27, 9.34, 18.65].

Kṛṣṇa makes clear that He needs nothing [3.22]. He acts in this world to set a proper example [3.23–24] and to establish the just rule of Law, *dharma* [4.7–8]. He institutes *yajña*, sacred offering, for that purpose—for our moral and spiritual development—not to exploit us. What in the world would God possibly do with our infinitesimal offerings?

Consider how most ordinary families operate. A mother teaches her children to give their father a birthday gift (which the parents themselves usually pay for). Dad then teaches the children to honor their mother's birthday. This is not parental vanity. Rather, devoted parents civilize their children by teaching them the ways of duty and love. The supreme parent does the same. It starts at the top.

However or wherever we choose to make an offering, Kṛṣṇa governs the offering and does so from within our body [8.4].

---

[2] *Enjoyer* translates the Sanskrit word *bhoktā*, which can also mean the one who possesses, rules, experiences, and consumes.

Kṛṣṇa pervades this entire world,[3] but is especially present in our hearts [13.18, 15.15, 18.61], from where He offers guidance—or, if we prefer, ignorance [15.15, 4.11].

We are like leaves that only live and flourish while joined to the tree from which they grew. By offering our work-fruits to Kṛṣṇa, we rejoin Him and again flourish as eternal beings. By spiritual *yajña* we link to all existence by linking to its Source, for Kṛṣṇa causes all beings to be [9.5, 10.15].

Pure souls devote all their acts to the supreme [9.27] and thus fully dissolve *karma* [4.23], transcending a world replete with karmic sensors and fetters. One then acts not as lord of the world, but as a devoted instrument of the supreme will [11.33], spiritualizing soul and body [4.26–27, 5.11].

This is possible because matter and spirit are Kṛṣṇa's inferior and superior energies [7.4–5]. Everything flows from Kṛṣṇa; He is the source of all [10.8]. Being thus part of God, matter and spirit have an original spiritual nature that manifests in direct contact with their Source, Kṛṣṇa. *Yajña* forges this transformative link.

To illustrate this process, ancient teachers cite the example of spark and fire. A spark springs from fire and thus burns and glows like fire. But when a spark falls out of the fire, the spark loses its fiery nature. Returning to fire, the spark again blazes.

Souls are like sparks. God is the original fire. Linked to God (*yoga*), we manifest our godly nature. Falling away from God, our godly nature vanishes until we again link to our Source. Even material objects like food or body act spiritually when offered to God [4.25–30] in devotion.

Kṛṣṇa explicitly describes the transformative power of *yajña* using the *classical* language of offering. Throughout the ancient world, people offered oblations to sacred fire, thus linking to divine power, however conceived. Kṛṣṇa uses the

---

[3] 6.30, 9.3, 13.28–29.

terms *oblation* and *fire*, literally and symbolically, to describe the transformative power of offering. Here Kṛṣṇa deploys the key word *brahman*. Vedic literature[4] often uses the term *brahman* to indicate the Absolute, the Universal Spirit, the eternal ground of all existence or the individual spiritual self (*atman*).

Thus Kṛṣṇa states that in a spiritual offering—an offering to *brahman*—the offered object (the oblation) is also *brahman*. Further, it is *brahman* fire that accepts the *brahman* offering. And the person who offers is also *brahman*. Thus by full focus (*samādhi*) on *brahman*-action (the offering), the offering soul surely achieves *brahman* [4.24].

By itself, this somewhat cryptic verse might lead one to some sort of monistic conclusion. After all, everything is the same thing: *brahman*. Further, the word *brahman* here is neither masculine nor feminine, but is grammatically neuter—a type of "it" word. Thus one might assume that the One (*brahman*) is impersonal.

However, when we place verse 4.24 in the context of the entire *Bhagavad-gītā*, a very different portrait emerges of *brahman* and its relation to Kṛṣṇa. God and soul are both *brahman* (as stated in 4.24); but Kṛṣṇa is the *Supreme Brahman* [10.12]. Moreover, ordinary *brahman*—not *Supreme Brahman*—rests on Kṛṣṇa [14.27].

Arjuna further clarifies the matter in chapter eight, where he directly asks Kṛṣṇa: "What is that *brahman*" [8.1]? Kṛṣṇa replies: "*Brahman* is the supreme imperishable; its nature is Higher Self" [8.3].

So *brahman*'s first characteristic—that it never perishes—sets it apart from all material objects, which all perish in time. Ephemeral items never endure and eternal things never

---

[4] Especially the *Upaniṣads*, *Brahma-sūtras*, commentaries on these works and the philosophical portions of *Mahā-bhārata*.

perish [2.16]. Further, *brahman* has a *sva-bhāva*, a personal nature as *adhyātman*, Higher Self [8.3].[5]

Here a theological pattern emerges that pervades the *Gītā*, as we will see in the next section. This pattern displays two fundamental concepts:

1. God and souls are one. In this case, they are both *brahman*, but God is still greater, being the *Supreme Brahman*.
2. God and soul are ultimately personal. Kṛṣṇa explicitly defines *brahman*'s nature as *Higher Self*, not as a state in which self dissolves into eternal impersonality.

The *Gītā* indicates in other ways that apparently impersonal language ultimately refers to the person Kṛṣṇa. Even in English we may describe a person with apparently impersonal terms like "a force to be reckoned with," "a veritable institution," "the team's anchor," etc. One can also describe a personal God in English with impersonal attributes: God is Truth (truth is not a gendered word), God is my rock and foundation, God is my path, etc.

Similarly, apart from *brahman* references, Kṛṣṇa refers to Himself in the neuter as *jñeyam*, the "Knowable" in six verses [13.13–18]. Here too, context makes clear that the neuter *Knowable* is a person. For example: "Its hands and feet are everywhere—everywhere, Its eyes, heads, mouths; It hears everywhere in the world and remains covering all" [13.14].

So although verse 4.24 identifies various offering components with *brahman*: fire, oblation, the offering act, etc., Kṛṣṇa

---

[5] The words *higher self* translate the Sanskrit *adhyātman*, composed of *adhi*, "over, above, higher," and *ātman*, "self, soul." The word *ātman* is often used alone to indicate the eternal self or soul. But since Sanskrit also uses *ātman* as a reflexive pronoun (as, for example, in *ātma-kṛtaḥ*, "self-made"), the prefix *adhi*, "over, above," etc. is sometimes added to *ātman* to emphasize that one refers to the eternal self, or soul.

later revisits these same components, stating that He, Kṛṣṇa, is actually all these things. Thus Kṛṣṇa is the offering, the *mantra*, the oblation, the fire, etc. [9.16].

I will show rather elaborately in the next section why and how Kṛṣṇa identifies Himself with material objects like fire and butter. In the meantime, consider Kṛṣṇa's use of the word *arpaṇam*, offering. It is this word that starts us off at 4.24, where Kṛṣṇa speaks of a "*brahman*-offering" (*brahma-arpaṇam*). Kṛṣṇa brings back this word *arpaṇam* at 9.27, where He declares: "Whatever you do, eat, offer or gift . . . make it an *offering* (*arpaṇam*) to Me." Thus the offering to *brahman* turns out to be an offering to Kṛṣṇa. This is not monism. God and soul are distinct: the soul worships; God is worshiped.

To grasp this central topic of the *Gītā*—the nature of God and God's relationship with souls—we will go deep into the *Gītā*'s original Sanskrit language, which I will translate for the reader in the most simple, direct, literal sense of each word. Few are fluent in Sanskrit and my intention is to do all I can to bring the reader as close as possible to the original text. Those who prefer highly esoteric, non-literal renderings of words should at least know what they are rendering, lest they render the words senseless. After all, if anything can mean anything, everything ultimately means nothing. Some people may find this thought encouraging, but we can hardly count Kṛṣṇa among them.

Let us then carefully consider the nature of God in God's Song, the *Bhagavad-gītā*.

PART VI
God (Kṛṣṇa)

Features of God

Bhagavad-gītā stresses several features of God. I will first list then briefly describe the main ones:

1. God is one.
2. God is the source of all.
3. God is fair and not jealous.
4. God loves us.
5. Creator and creation are one and different (this particular feature will be elaborately discussed in the following section on *vibhūti*, God's expansive being).

God is One

One often hears the claim that among major world religions, only the Abrahamic traditions[1] emphasize monotheism. And yet, *Bhagavad-gītā*, perhaps the most revered single text of South Asia, teaches that one supreme absolute God (Kṛṣṇa) creates, maintains, contains, rules and pervades all worlds. As Kṛṣṇa Himself says: "There is nothing beyond Me; all this world rests on Me like pearls strung on thread" [7.7].

---

[1]Judaism, Christianity and Islam, in various forms, trace their monotheism back to the patriarch Abraham.

Upon seeing the Lord's cosmic form, Arjuna says to Kṛṣṇa: "You are the world's Father . . . You have no equal, whence one superior? . . . Your power is beyond compare" [11.44]. Indeed, Arjuna sees the entire universe within Kṛṣṇa's cosmic body [11.7].

Arjuna sees all gods within Kṛṣṇa's cosmic body [11.15], and even sees god-communities begging for mercy as they rush into Kṛṣṇa's all-devouring form of Time [11.32]. Themselves mortal [8.16], the gods can offer but temporary rewards [7.23]. Thus only those whose selfish desires rob them of reason worship gods (not God) [7.20], whether those gods be found in religious texts, Hollywood movies, rock concerts, halls of political power or on athletic fields. Even those focused on the material mode of virtue, rather than pure spirituality, worship gods [17.4] that are themselves entwined in material modes [18.40].

Indeed the gods cannot understand Kṛṣṇa's personal form, for God alone fully knows Himself [10.14–15]. They do, however, always yearn to see His personal form [11.52]. Lord of gods [11.37], Kṛṣṇa has no equal or superior [11.43].

According to well-known Hindu teachings, the god Brahmā creates the world, Viṣṇu sustains it, and Śiva destroys it. But, in fact, Kṛṣṇa (Viṣṇu) Himself ultimately performs all three functions directly [9.18]—or indirectly through His agents.

Arjuna literally *sees* Kṛṣṇa's supremacy in the cosmic vision of Chapter Eleven, which I will discuss in detail further on.

God is the Source of All

Kṛṣṇa states: "I am the source of all; everything emanates from Me" [10.8]. The gods do not know Kṛṣṇa's origin, for He is their origin [10.2]. He is the original God [11.38], the source of our memory and knowledge [15.15]. Indeed, whatever beautiful or powerful being exists in this world displays but a spark of

God's splendor [10.41]. Arjuna tells Kṛṣṇa: "You encompass all, and thus You are all" [11.40].

Time itself, which drives all things to their destiny, is Kṛṣṇa [10.32], as He dramatically shows Arjuna in Chapter Eleven. At creation's end, all creatures that did not end their *karma* come to rest in Him, only to be cast again into the world at the next creation [9.7]. Indeed Kṛṣṇa sends forth and withdraws the entire universe [7.6].

God is Fair and Not Jealous

Fortunately, with all His infinite power, Kṛṣṇa fairly reciprocates with each of us [4.11]. We may ignore Kṛṣṇa, yet whatever else we admire or adore is but a small sample of His creative art [10.41]. Thus the devotee of nature, art, philosophy, love or science factually honors a single aspect of God's creation. In that sense, as Kṛṣṇa explains, everyone pursues God in their own way [4.11]. Equal to all, He does not favor or hate anyone; though with proper reciprocation, He abides in those who abide in Him [9.29].

God respects our free will. At the *Gītā's* end He tells Arjuna: "Fully reflect on this teaching and do as you wish" [18.63]. Yet Kṛṣṇa is not indifferent to our happiness. In the very next verse He says: "I will speak for your good, for I love you very much" [18.63]. After all, we are all part of Him [15.7].

Thankfully, as the *Gītā* informs us, we do not suffer under the jealous rage of a possessive God. To the contrary, Kṛṣṇa fixes our faith in whatever object we choose to worship [7.21]. He alone then grants our wishes by means of our chosen deity [7.22]. Why?

Like any good parent, God encourages His children's education. After all, we must have full knowledge of this world if we are to transcend it. We ourselves must *see* the difference between godly and godless life. God helps us to explore the universe, make our own comparisons, and decide reasonably what is in our ultimate interest.

Kṛṣṇa does not resent those who ignore Him, but simply gives them what they want and deserve [7.21]. Thus Kṛṣṇa says that those who cultivate worldly virtue tend to worship not God, but His deputed agents [17.4]: gods, angels, higher spirits, spiritual beings, or whatever a particular culture calls them. Nonetheless, Kṛṣṇa rewards virtue without imposing doctrinal requirements. Thus those who do not accept Kṛṣṇa but *do* cultivate virtue become wise [14.17] and happy [14.6], rising to higher states [14.18] and worlds [14.14].

Of course, mundane virtue's rewards are temporary, as is the universe. Is God thus still coercing us to choose Him by *imposing mortality* on those who ignore Him? Not really. Worldly pleasures end because they arise not from true eternal self, but from self's covering, the body. Even virtuous self-delusion cannot endure forever, for it is based on what does not truly exist: self without God, or self as a material body. Thus those sworn to gods go to gods, those sworn to ancestors go to them, and those devoted to God, Kṛṣṇa, go to Him [9.25]. Ancestors and gods hold mortal posts and offer mortal rewards. *Caveat emptor.*

This vision of life respects individual choice, unlike the somewhat coercive view that we all go to the same place no matter what our choice, or the highly coercive view that unspeakably horrible consequences await even nice people who do not join the "*right*" religion. We find neither extreme in the *Gītā*, which describes Kṛṣṇa as a supreme friend, not a jealous angry God. Kṛṣṇa encourages us to accept Him, but if we don't, we get results that fairly match the moral quality of our intentions and actions [14.8]. Any form of religion that promotes goodness is accepted as a step on the path.

The awakened do not delight in temporary pleasures born of contact between physical bodies and the physical world [5.22].

Rather by embracing eternal self, one finds far greater joy, concluding that there is no greater gain [6.22].

God Loves Us

Kṛṣṇa creates a teleological cosmos—i.e., a universe with objective purpose: to guide us to pure goodness and liberation. Nature is a cosmic womb in which Kṛṣṇa, the *seed-giving Father*, places all wandering souls [14.4]. Kṛṣṇa is our supreme father and mother [9.17, 11.43, 14.4]. And like any loving parent, He is our biggest fan, urging us to pursue our highest good. We find real peace by accepting Him as the kind-hearted friend of all beings [5.29]. Unlike the often-peevish Greek gods of Homer, Kṛṣṇa neither hates nor favors any soul. Like any loving parent, He is equal to all His children [9.29]. He personally uplifts those who turn to Him for shelter [12.7], forgiving all offenses [18.66] and bestowing supreme peace and eternal abode [18.62]. Kṛṣṇa considers one who simply studies His dialogue with Arjuna in *Bhagavad-gītā* to have honored Him by "knowledge-*yoga*" [18.70]. Kṛṣṇa speaks to Arjuna, who represents us all, for the Lord dearly loves him [18.64].[2]

God's Expansive Being (*Vibhūti*)

In this section, we look more closely at Kṛṣṇa's relation to matter, which He calls His "lesser nature" [7.4]. You may recall that Kṛṣṇa declared that even material articles of offering are *brahman* [4.24], and that Kṛṣṇa later identified Himself with those same articles, saying, for example, that "I alone am the clarified-butter oblation, I am the fire . . ." etc. [9.16].

Moreover, Kṛṣṇa states that after many births, one with knowledge sees that Kṛṣṇa is everything [7.19]. And, as noted

---

[2] My old friend, Professor Graham Schweig, writes eloquently on this last point in the introduction to his own translation of *Bhagavad-gītā*.

above, Arjuna tells Kṛṣṇa, "You encompass all; and thus You are all" [11.40].

In *Bhagavad-gītā*, Kṛṣṇa identifies Himself with many objects and qualities in this world, in each case simply saying *I am* the respective object or quality. In Sanskrit, He normally uses the pronoun *aham* ("I") or the verb *asmi* ("am").[3] Here is another typical example: "I am the taste in water . . . the light of moon and sun,[4] sacred *Om* in all Vedas, sound in space, valor in men" [7.8].

These "*identity verses*," as I call them, number about thirty, and mostly occur in Chapters Seven [7.8–11] and Ten [10.19–38]. Such statements have led some casual readers to conclude that *Bhagavad-gītā* teaches a sort of pantheism: the doctrine that the physical universe *is* God and that there is no separate, personal God apart from the universe.

Other readers see in this language some type of monism, such as the unqualified claim that "God is all, and all is God." However, a closer look at these *identity verses*, in which Kṛṣṇa claims to be various features of the material world, will make clear what He is actually saying. In my analysis of the *identity verses*, I will first provide the categories of objects with which Kṛṣṇa identifies Himself, and then show how He actually explains His own statements.

In verses 7.8–11, Kṛṣṇa identifies Himself with the following types of objects:

1. **Essence of beings:** Kṛṣṇa is the life and perennial seed of all beings.

---

[3] In Sanskrit, as in other languages, such as Spanish, Portuguese, Italian, etc., a conjugated verb standing alone implies the pronoun. But, unlike those languages, a pronoun standing alone implies the verb *to be*. Thus in Sanskrit, *aham asmi* means *I am*, but one may convey the same meaning, though less emphatically, with just *aham* (I) or just *asmi* (am).

[4] See also 13.18.

2. **Virtues in people:** Kṛṣṇa is valor in men, austerity of the austere, reason of the rational, splendor of the splendid, unselfish strength of the strong and desire consonant with Dharma.

3. **Traits of nature:** Kṛṣṇa is taste in water, the light of moon and sun,[5] sound in space, pure fragrance in earth and splendor in fire.

4. **Sacred objects:** Kṛṣṇa is the sacred syllable *Om*[6] in all Vedas.

What does all this mean? Kṛṣṇa makes that clear, for He frames these *identity verses* [7.8–11] with what I call "*origin verses*," which He places both before and after them: verses declaring that Kṛṣṇa is the *origin* of the objects and qualities that He claims to *be*. Thus Kṛṣṇa identifies with those objects and qualities in the sense that they are *His* creations, with the Creator being both one with and different from the creation. To make this clearer, let us look at the *origin verses* for 7.8–11.

In Chapter Seven, immediately preceding the *identity verses*, Kṛṣṇa declares that matter is His inferior *separated* energy [7.4] and that souls are His superior *living* energy [7.5]. These two energies are the *source* of all creatures—who are, after all, souls in material bodies—and Kṛṣṇa is the *source* of these two energies. Thus Kṛṣṇa is the origin and dissolution of the entire cosmos [7.6], not to speak of objects within it. Indeed there is nothing beyond Him, and all this world rests on Him like pearls strung on thread [7.7]. The objects of the world are not fully God; rather they emanate from and rest on Him. In *that* sense, they are one with their Maker and Sustainer.

Moreover, within the *identity verses* [7.8–11] themselves, Kṛṣṇa states: "Know Me as the perennial seed (*bīja*) of all beings" [7.10]. *Bīja*, seed, also means "primary cause or principle,

---

[5] See also 15.12–13.

[6] See also 9.17.

origin" [MW]. Thus powerful *origin verses* both precede and inform the *identity verses.*

Finally, completing the frame, a strong *origin verse* concludes this section of Chapter Seven: "Know that all virtuous, passionate and dark states *come from Me alone. I am not in them. They are in Me*" [7.12 (emphasis mine)].[7] Since the three material modes—virtue, passion and darkness—permeate all material things [10.39], Kṛṣṇa is clearly saying that *all* states in the universe come from Him. Thus explicit *origin verses* can be seen to frame the *identity verses.*

Kṛṣṇa is teaching that Creator and creation are one but different (the fifth feature of God mentioned in the previous subsection). To help us grasp this, traditional scholars often cite the analogy of sun and sunshine: In one sense, the sun is present in sunshine. Thus sun and sunshine is one thing: *sun shining.* And yet, fortunately for us, all the sun's heat and light is not present in the sunshine that warms and lights our world. Conclusion: sun is both one with and different from its rays. God is like the sun and His creation is like the sun's rays: one and different at the same time.

Indeed, later in this same Chapter Seven, Kṛṣṇa states that after many births, one who knows Him to be everything comes to Him for shelter [7.19]. Thus knowledge that God is everything leads not to declaring oneself God, but rather to submitting to the Supreme.

In Chapter Ten, Kṛṣṇa gives a much larger set of *identity* verses [10.19–38], with a few repeats and some additional categories. Here He even more powerfully frames these with *origin verses.* I will again first list categories of identification and then provide the framing *origin verses.*

Kṛṣṇa identifies Himself with the following in 10.19–38:

---

[7] Kṛṣṇa makes the same point at 9.4.

1. **Essence of beings:** Kṛṣṇa is the soul in every being's heart; the start, middle and end of beings;[8] consciousness of beings; seed[9] of all beings; mind among senses.[10]
2. **Virtues in people:** Kṛṣṇa is the wisdom of the wise; of feminine things, He is fame, beauty, speech, memory, reason, firmness and forgiveness; He is splendor of the splendid, goodness of the good, right conduct of those seeking victory and the monarch among men.
3. **Traits of nature:**[11] Kṛṣṇa is the radiant sun among luminaries; of water bodies, the ocean; of mountain ranges, the Himalayan; of all trees, the fig; of beasts, the king of beasts (lion); wind of purifiers, the shark of great fish; of rivers, the Ganges; of months, Trailhead;[12] of seasons, flower-source spring.
4. **Sacred objects:** Kṛṣṇa is *Sāma-veda* of Vedas;[13] of sounds, the one that does not perish;[14] of offerings, the quiet chant; of hymns, the great hymn;[15] *Gāyatrī* of metered chants; of sciences, the spiritual science.[16]

The following categories are found only in Chapter Ten:

5. **Cosmic forces:** Kṛṣṇa is Time among driving forces;[17] He is unperishing Time, all-facing Creator, all-taking

[8] See also 9.19.

[9] See also 9.18.

[10] In the *Gītā's* psychology, mind is the cognitive faculty that likes and dislikes and also coordinates sense activities.

[11] See also 15.14.

[12] Trailhead indicates Mārga–śīrṣa: November–December.

[13] *Sāma-veda* is the Veda of Chants, one of the primeval Veda scriptures (see also 9.17).

[14] "The one that does not perish" is another reference to the sacred syllable *Om* (see also 8.13, 9.17, 17.23–24).

[15] The great hymn refers to the *bṛhat-sāman* [10.35], a famous Vedic hymn.

[16] See also 9.2 and 9.16.

[17] See also 11.32.

Death, the coming forth of all that will come, the beginning, middle and end of creations.

6. **Verbal traits:** of those making claims, Kṛṣṇa is the conclusion; He is "*a*" among letters, the pair among linguistic compounds.
7. **Social traits:** Kṛṣṇa is dicing among deceivers, the rod among subduers, and silence of secrets.
8. **The best of celestial groups:** Kṛṣṇa is Viṣṇu of Ādityas, Marīci of Maruts, Moon of *nakṣatras*, Indra of gods, Śaṅkara of Rudras, Kuvera of Yakṣa-Rakṣas, Vāyu of Vasus, begetter Cupid, Prahlāda of Daityas, Vāsudeva of Vṛṣṇis, Arjuna of Pāṇḍavas.
9. **A celestial or divine paragon of groups that include celestials and humans:** Kṛṣṇa is Skanda of military leaders, Citraratha of Gandharvas, Ananta of Nāgas, Varuṇa of aquatics, Aryamā of forefathers, Yama of controllers, Rāma of weapon-bearers.
10. **Celestial exemplars of nature (here Kṛṣṇa identifies with a celestial object as an exemplar of a natural category also found on earth):** Kṛṣṇa is Meru[18] among mountains; of horses, nectar-born Uccaiḥ-śravas;[19] Airāvata[20] of lordly elephants, Vajra[21] of weapons; of cows, Kāma-dhuk;[22] Vāsuki[23] of serpents, Garuḍa[24] of winged creatures.

---

[18] Meru is a wonderfully high mountain around which the planets revolve.

[19] Uccaiḥ-śravas is the Sun god's horse.

[20] Airāvata is Lord Indra's elephant.

[21] Vajra is Lord Indra's fabulous thunderbolt weapon.

[22] Kāma-dhuk is Sage Vasiṣṭha's mystic cow that yields all desires.

[23] Vāsuki is a celestial serpent-king.

[24] Garuḍa is the divine eagle that carries Lord Viṣṇu.

11. **Priests and sages:** Kṛṣṇa is Bṛhaspati of priests, Bhṛgu of great sages, Nārada of god-sages, Sage Kapila of perfected beings, Vyāsa of seers, Uśanā of sages.

In Chapter Ten, Kṛṣṇa frames twenty *identity verses* with a full eleven *origin verses*, beginning with these: Kṛṣṇa is the *origin* of gods and great sages [10.2]; He has no origin [10.3]; the various states of beings come from Him [10.4–5]; great sages and Manus[25] are born from His mind [10.6]; we should learn in truth His *yoga* (mystic power) and *vibhūti* (glory) [10.7], for *He is the source of everything and everything emanates from Him* [10.8 (my emphasis)].

After the *identity verses* [10.19–38], Kṛṣṇa again completes the frame, saying that He is the *bīja* (seed, primary cause, principle or *origin*) of all beings [10.39].[26] He asks us to understand: "Each and every being that possesses glory, beauty or true excellence springs from a portion of My splendor" [10.41]; indeed, "with a single portion of Myself, I steadily sustain this entire universe" [10.42].

Kṛṣṇa identifies with the world because He infuses it with His own glory. Yet He stands above and sustains it: "*I am not in them; they are in Me*" [7.12 (my emphasis)]. Creator and creation are one yet different.

In verse 10.7, Kṛṣṇa uses a key term for the first time: *vibhūti*. So important is *vibhūti* to this discussion, that I will explain it further. I translate *vibhūti* as *glory*, but that only begins to explain this Sanskrit word.

In the word *vi-bhūti*, the prefix *vi-* indicates differentiation, distribution, diffusion or expansion and *bhūti* (from the root *bhū*) means being, existence (especially flourishing existence), prosperity, might, power, fortune, etc. The composite *vi-bhūti* thus indicates flourishing mighty existence that *expands,*

---

[25] Manus are the original patriarchs and lawgivers of humankind.

[26] Kṛṣṇa also states this at 9.18 and 14.4.

multiplies and pervades—and hence *might, greatness, superhuman power, splendor, glory, magnificence,* etc.

In Chapter Ten, Kṛṣṇa explains that He is the source of gods, sages and, indeed, all states of being in this world. He calls this remarkable power His *vibhūti* (expansive might, etc.) and His *yoga* (mystic power) [10.7]. After hearing Kṛṣṇa's glories, and glorifying Him in turn, Arjuna asks to hear more about Kṛṣṇa's *vibhūti*[s]. Here is a very literal, if not literary, translation of Arjuna's request:

"You ought to explain completely Your divine personal *vibhūti*[s], the *vibhūti*[s] by which You . . . pervade these worlds [10.16]; describe extensively Your . . . *vibhūti*" [10.18].

The Lord replies: "Yes, I will describe My divine personal *vibhūti*[s] . . ." [10.19].

Immediately after this, at 10.20, the *identity verses* begin. So, for example, when Kṛṣṇa says, "Of trees I am the holy fig tree" [10.26], we should not conclude that every holy fig tree on earth is the original God, but rather that this type tree is an exemplary *vibhūti*, an expansion of Kṛṣṇa's flourishing creative might and being.

After Arjuna repeatedly asks to hear about His *vibhūti*[s], Kṛṣṇa says that He will describe them. Then, at chapter's end, Kṛṣṇa says that He has just given "an example of My *vibhūti*'s extent, for there is no end to My divine *vibhūti*[s]" [10.40]. Indeed ". . . each and every being that has *vibhūti* (glory, etc.), beauty or true excellence, springs from a part of My splendor" [10.41].

Again, Creator is one with creation, yet each glorious creation is but a small part of the Creator's infinite glory. Thus there is not a hint in the *Gītā* that Kṛṣṇa is actually Arjuna, that Arjuna is Kṛṣṇa, that they are one person or one impersonal object, that their individuality is illusion, or that Arjuna has any other ultimate duty or wish than to serve his Lord with devotion.

Further, Kṛṣṇa describes material nature as His inferior energy, below the living souls who animate it [7.4–5]. Kṛṣṇa oversees nature, causing it to act [9.10]. Those who take shelter in Him cross over His illusory material nature [7.14]. Nature is not God; it belongs to God.

The Supreme Person (*Parama-Puruṣaḥ*)

Having considered Kṛṣṇa's relation to material nature, let us now precisely evaluate His relation to other souls. Here too we will clearly see that He is simultaneously one with and different from all other souls.

Thinkers in all the world's major religions have long debated whether God is ultimately personal or impersonal. Our own destiny hangs in the balance: if God, our creator or emanator, is originally and ultimately impersonal, then we are most likely also ultimately impersonal; if, on the other hand, we flow from a personal loving God, then our personal loving nature, at its very best, is really us.

Those who value free, individual, personal life, in loving relation with other free persons, will be glad to hear that *Bhagavad-gītā* steadily teaches that both soul and God are eternal individual persons.

Kṛṣṇa states from the start that both God and souls have always existed, and always will exist, as individual beings [2.12]. And He regularly calls the individual soul a person (*puruṣa*).[27] Many verses also speak of Kṛṣṇa as a *puruṣa*, person. In that sense, souls and God are one. But they are also different.

Kṛṣṇa is the *Ultimate* Person (*uttama puruṣa*) [8.1, 10.15, 11.3], *Supreme* Person (*paraḥ puruṣaḥ*) [8.22, 13.23], *Supreme Divine* Person (*paramam*, or *param, puruṣam divyam*) [8.8, 8.10], *Everlasting Divine* Person (*puruṣaṁ śāśvatam divyam*) [10.12],

[27] 2.15, 2.21, 2.60, 3.4, 9.3, 13.20–22, 13.24 and 17.3; Arjuna: 13.1.

Eternal Person (*sanātanaḥ puruṣaḥ*) [11.18], the *Ancient* Person (*purāṇaḥ puruṣaḥ*) [11.38] and the *Original* Person (*ādyam puruṣam*) [15.4]. We souls are persons precisely because we are part of the Supreme Person [15.7].

Similarly, we are *ātmā*, self or soul, as declared everywhere in the *Gītā*, because we are part of Kṛṣṇa, the *Supreme* Self or Soul (*paramātmā*) [6.7, 13.23, 15.17]. Again, God and soul are one and different.

Yet some believe that Kṛṣṇa is an impersonal formless Being that takes on a visible form when descending to this world as an *avatāra*. In this view, the person Kṛṣṇa merely represents in our world what is ultimately a nameless, formless impersonal Truth.

Kṛṣṇa, however, explicitly denies this: "Not knowing My supreme nature, the unwise think that formless being takes on visible individuality" [7.24].

And lest we presume that Kṛṣṇa teaches primitive anthropomorphism, He states that His personal form is *acintya* [8.9], inconceivable to unaided human reason. It is knowable only through pure devotion [11.54]. Even celestial beings, by their own mental powers, do not understand the Lord's individual form [10.14].

Indeed it is as a Supreme Person that Kṛṣṇa pervades this world and is present within all beings [8.22, 13.23]. That Eternal Divine Person is the supreme absolute *brahman* [10.12], the Ultimate Person who causes existing things to exist [10.15].

Again, it is precisely as the Supreme *Person* that Kṛṣṇa both pervades [6.29, 9.4, 11.38, 13.29] and contains [6.29, 9.6] all that is, for He is *nidhāna*, the *receptacle* [9.18]—indeed *paraṁ nidhānam*, the *supreme receptacle* [11.18, 11.38].

Yet even His containment of all existence is not impersonal, for He is *nivāsa*, the *abode* or *home* of all [11.25, 11.37]. Arjuna calls Kṛṣṇa *jagan-nivāsa*, abode of the universe [11.37, 11.45]. The idea is clear: even if we ignore or deny Kṛṣṇa, our true home is always with and within Him. He is the "great Lord of all worlds" [5.29].

Arjuna directly asks Kṛṣṇa, which of two groups best understands *yoga*: those devoted to Kṛṣṇa as a person or those devoted to an imperceptible truth [12.1], beyond description and inconceivable [12.3].

The Lord replies that those who worship Him rather than the imperceptible are more advanced in *yoga* [12.2–4]. In fact, the impersonalist ultimately comes to Kṛṣṇa, but by a far more troublesome path [12.5].

Advanced spiritual practice does not obliterate personal self, but rather restores its true godly state. Within the *Gītā*, there is no project, plan or idea to annihilate the personal self—to merge into divine corporate radiance. Liberation means to exalt, not destroy, one's self.

Kṛṣṇa does not reveal Himself to all [7.25]. He reciprocates fairly with everyone [4.11] and only those who love Him purely can see Him [11.54]. Thus those without spiritual understanding do not recognize Him as the unperishing Unborn [7.25]. Not knowing His supreme nature, they believe that God is impersonal and invisible but has taken on (or entered) a *vyakti*, a visible personal form [7.24].

Arjuna states: "Oh Lord, neither gods nor the godless understand Your manifest Personality" [10.14].

Kṛṣṇa clarifies that God, the Divine Person, exists with form: a body that is inconceivable, sun-colored and smaller than an atom [8.9], yet infinite [11.16, 11.38, 11.47], cosmic [11.16], majestic [11.3, 11.9], astonishing [11.20], made of splendor, original, revealed by the Lord's own mystic power [11.47] and resembling that of a human being [11.51]. Only those with pure devotion are able to know, approach and actually see the Lord as Arjuna did [11.53–54].

One might suspect that there is a still higher truth beyond a personal God, but Kṛṣṇa puts that doubt to rest: "[Those] who know Me as the Ultimate Person, know all, and devote themselves to Me with all their being" [15.19].

This understanding is most advanced scripture, and to understand this is to really understand [15.20]. Thus we are eternal persons because we emanate from [10.8] and are part of [15.7] an eternal infinite Person.

As mentioned in the section on sacrifice, we eternal souls are *brahman* (spirit) and can regain our *brahman* existence;[28] but Kṛṣṇa is the foundation of *brahman* [14.27], the Supreme *Brahman* [10.12]. The point is clear.

Such Sanskrit terms as *brahman*, *puruṣa* and *ātman* are used for both God and soul, with God being the superlative in each category. However, there are several terms reserved exclusively for souls. Let us now look at these.

Terms Reserved for Souls (*Bhūta, Jīva, Dehī*)

Bhūta

Kṛṣṇa often refers to souls in bodies as *bhūta* (plural *bhūtāni*), which I translate as *being*, in the sense of *a living being*. Although Kṛṣṇa is certainly a being, the *Gītā* never refers to Him as *bhūta*, and we shall see why.

The word *bhūta* comes from the verbal root *bhū*, which means *to be*, but also often means *to become*. In this sense, *bhūta* means *one who has come to be*—i.e., *one who has become*. The *Gītā* makes clear early on that both God and individual souls have always existed [2.12]. Thus what *comes to be* is not soul itself, but rather soul's ephemeral *persona*, produced when soul enters body. Kṛṣṇa directly states that a *bhūta* arises when matter and spirit combine [7.4–6].

---

[28] 2.72, 4.24, 5.20, 5.24, 6.27, 14.26, 18.53–54, etc.

One may literally translate 8.19–20 as follows: "This very group, those who have come to be, after repeatedly becoming . . . are helplessly dissolved. [There is, however,] another superior state that does not perish when all who have become are perishing."

Since Kṛṣṇa time and again states that souls never perish, clearly what perishes here is the composite identity formed when soul enters body. Thus our identity as woman, man, dog, bird or tree arises when a living, conscious soul animates an otherwise dead material body, creating thereby a living, temporary creature—a *bhūta*. This composite *persona* is literally dissolved when soul leaves body.

Yet, since Kṛṣṇa does not take on a material body, He is not a *bhūta*. His identity as Kṛṣṇa does not *come to be* like *our* worldly identities. Kṛṣṇa has always been Kṛṣṇa [2.12] and will forever be Kṛṣṇa, the Supreme Divine Person.

Bound to a material body, a *bhūta* must follow nature [3.33]. The *bhūta* seeks freedom from nature [13.35]. Kṛṣṇa controls nature [9.10]. He is not a *bhūta*. The *Gītā* never states that His body, or His identity, comes to be.

The *Gītā* describes Kṛṣṇa's relation to *bhūta*s (to souls like us), whose temporary identity does come to be. Kṛṣṇa is a kind-hearted friend to every *bhūta* [5.29], eternal seed of every *bhūta* [7.10]. He knows every *bhūta*, past, present and future [7.26]. He is the great Lord of *bhūtas* [9.11], and their origin [9.13]. He is equal to every *bhūta* [9.29, 13.28] and, as the master, causes all *bhūtas* to be [10.15]. He is the beginning, middle and end of *bhūtas* [10.20], and their preserver [13.17]. He sustains *bhūta*s by His power [15.13], for He is their Lord [18.61]. And at eon's end, the *bhūta* enters Kṛṣṇa's own nature [9.7].

The conclusion: as souls, as persons, as parts of God, we are one with Him. Yet we are also different. In this world, we do business as *bhūtas*. Kṛṣṇa does not.

The *Gītā* employs other important terms to indicate souls, but not God.

Jīva

The word *jīva* ("life, living") usually indicates "the personal or living soul, as distinguished from the universal soul . . ." [MW]. Similarly, the term *jīvātman* ("living soul") indicates "the living or personal or individual soul as distinct from the *paramātman*, the Supreme Soul" [MW]. The *Gītā* twice calls the soul *jīva-bhūta* (living being) [7.5, 15.7], but never uses this term for God.

The *Gītā* also uses for individual souls, but never for God, several terms relating to our bodies.

Dehin, Śarīrin, Deha-bhṛt, Dehavad

Bhagavad-gītā's most common word for "body" is *deha*. And eleven times[29] the *Gītā* calls the soul *dehin*, "one who *has* a body" or "the embodied." Thus soul is distinct from body. Another word for body is *śarīra*, and the soul is called *śarīrin* [2.18], "one who *has* a body" or "the embodied." The *Gītā* also describes the soul as *deha-bhṛt*, "one who bears a body" [8.4, 14.14, 18.11], and *dehavad*, "one who has a body" [12.5]. Kṛṣṇa twice uses the word *kalevara*, also meaning *body*, to describe how the soul gives up a material body at death [8.5–6].

In the *Gītā*, all these Sanskrit terms—*dehin, śarīrin, deha-bhṛt, dehavad* and *kalevara*—clearly indicate a soul as distinct from its material body. Yet the *Gītā* uses none of these terms, nor any similar terms, to describe Kṛṣṇa. The *Gītā* gives no indication that Kṛṣṇa, the Supreme Soul [6.7, 13.23, 15.17], is different from His body. This is entirely consistent with our analysis of *bhūta*.

At the start, Kṛṣṇa tells us that we are eternal souls in temporary bodies [2.18, 2.20, 2.30]. Our body is matter (*aparā prakṛti*), the Lord's inferior energy; but we souls are *parā prakṛti*, the Lord's superior, living energy [7.4–5]. The *Gītā* never describes

---

[29] See 2.13, 2.22, 2.30, 2.59, 3.40, 5.13, 14.5, 14.7, 14.8, 14.20 and 17.2.

Kṛṣṇa's body as material, temporary or limited. Rather His form is *ananta*, infinite [11.16, 11.38].

Kṛṣṇa describes souls' transmigration from one body to another [2.13]. Souls give up old bodies as one gives up old, worn out clothes [2.22]. However, spiritual knowledge travels with the soul from one body to another. Thus spiritual practitioners regain spiritual knowledge "from a past body" [6.43]. Many verses describe the soul *giving up* or *letting go* of the body. However, none of this language is applied to Kṛṣṇa.

Kṛṣṇa and Arjuna both appeared in this world many times. The Lord recalls all these births, but Arjuna does not [4.5]. That is because Kṛṣṇa's birth and activities are divine [4.9].

Due to *karma*, ordinary souls accept and give up a physical body. But *karma* laws cannot affect Kṛṣṇa [4.14]; they cannot force Him to accept a material body, for He rules nature with all its laws [9.10].

Kṛṣṇa often states that He is within the soul's body, specifically in the heart.[30] But Kṛṣṇa never says that He is within His own body. There is no hint of Kṛṣṇa giving up His body or of His body taking birth or dying, as our bodies do.

A final point here: in the *Gītā*, Kṛṣṇa often speaks of bondage and freedom. With various noun and verb forms of the root *muc*, Kṛṣṇa teaches us of the soul's liberation from birth and death,[31] from *karma* [2.39, 3.31, 4.22–23, 9.28], from evil,[32] from anger, lust, fear, etc. [2.64, 5.26, 5.28, 16.22], from duality [7.28, 15.5, 12.15], from attachment [3.9, 18.26, 18.54], or simply from bondage [5.3]. And while one can easily compile a similar list of words indicating bondage, the *Gītā* nowhere hints that *Kṛṣṇa* is ever bound by or freed from *anything*. In the *Gītā* He is God—personally.

---

[30] Here is a sample of such verses: 8.2, 8.22, 13.23, 13.3, 13.16, 13.17, 13.28, 15.14, 15.15, 16.18 and 18.61.

[31] See 2.51, 4.9, 4.14, 5.17, 7.29, 8.21, 13.26, 15.4 and 14.20.

[32] See 3.13, 4.16, 9.1, 10.3, 18.66 and 18.71.

Clearly the *Gītā* teaches that God does not have a material body as we do. He is not a *bhūta*. He is never bound or freed. Yet Kṛṣṇa appeared in this world as a human (or humanlike) person. People saw Kṛṣṇa, embraced Him, spoke with Him. How are we to understand Kṛṣṇa's body? Here too, the *Gītā* comes to our rescue.

Kṛṣṇa's Original Form (*Rūpa*)

We saw that the *Gītā* calls the soul *dehī*, *śarīrī*, *deha-bhṛt* and *dehavad*, Sanskrit terms indicating one who is somehow separate or different from one's body. None of these Sanskrit terms describe Kṛṣṇa. The *Gītā* often describes how souls give up their bodies and take another. None of this applies to Kṛṣṇa. Nothing in the *Gītā* suggests that Kṛṣṇa is separate or different from His body. Kṛṣṇa often states that He is within the body of embodied souls—within their hearts. But Kṛṣṇa never states that He is within His own body. Unlike the soul's birth under the stringent laws of nature, Kṛṣṇa rules nature and takes divine birth by His own power [4.6].

In the *Gītā*, Kṛṣṇa appears to Arjuna in three different forms: His normal "sublime *humanlike* form" [11.50]; His form with four hands holding symbolic objects [11.46]; and His cosmic form [11.9–45].

Kṛṣṇa also tells Arjuna to meditate on the Supreme Divine Person as one who possesses an *inconceivable form* (*acintya-rūpa*), *colored like the sun*, *beyond darkness* [8.9].

If Kṛṣṇa's form is *acintya*, inconceivable, how then are we to understand it? The term *acintya*, inconceivable, does not mean *unknowable*. Thus Kṛṣṇa teaches that one can know many things about the soul, including the fact that souls are *acintya*, inconceivable [2.25]. In short, *acintya* indicates that which we *cannot know* by our own unaided powers, but which we *can know* by hearing from Kṛṣṇa, or from *tattva-darśi*[s], seers of truth [2.16, 4.34]. Thus we can know something of Kṛṣṇa's body if we hear from Kṛṣṇa. After all, only Kṛṣṇa truly knows Kṛṣṇa [10.15].

Bhagavad-gītā directly mentions Kṛṣṇa's body twenty-three times, and twenty-one times uses the word *rūpa*, a term the *Gītā* never uses for material bodies. *Rūpa* indicates "form, shape, figure," and may further mean "handsome form, loveliness, grace, beauty, splendor."[33]

Bhagavad-gītā's celebrated Chapter Eleven reveals Kṛṣṇa's cosmic form, by which He pervades, contains and consumes the universe. The *Gītā* says much more about the cosmic form than it does about the others, and many readers believe this wondrous body to be Kṛṣṇa's highest form. But textual evidence suggests otherwise. Let us therefore first consider Kṛṣṇa's spectacular cosmic form—what it means to Arjuna and its relation to Kṛṣṇa's other forms, including His *regular* form as Kṛṣṇa.

Arjuna pointedly asks to see Kṛṣṇa's cosmic form: ". . . O Supreme Lord, I want to see Your lordly form" [11.3]. To convey the impact of the original Sanskrit (*īśvara/aiśvara*), I use the cognate terms *Lord* and *lordly*. Arjuna addresses Kṛṣṇa as *parama-īśvara* (Supreme Lord), and then asks to see the *aiśvara* (lordly) form. Of course, *aiśvara*, lordly, is derived from *īśvara*, Lord.

A question arises: if Kṛṣṇa is Lord, and Arjuna has been talking to and seeing Kṛṣṇa for some time, why then ask to see the Lord's lordly form as if it were different from the form of Kṛṣṇa? Is Kṛṣṇa's humanlike form not the true form of God?

After seeing what he asked for—Kṛṣṇa's cosmic form, which overawes and overwhelms him, as it does many readers—Arjuna bows to Kṛṣṇa "from in front, from behind and from all sides" [11.40], and says: "Thinking You a *friend*, I imposed myself, not knowing this glory of Yours" [11.41].

---

[33] Monier-Williams Oxford Sanskrit Dictionary.

Here we glimpse an aspect of Kṛṣṇa that for millennia has charmed and mystified: the all-powerful, all-knowing God plays like a human being, forming such intimate friendships with His devotees that they forget He is God. Thus Arjuna goes on to say: "Just to tease, I insulted You, Acyuta, in sporting, resting, sitting and eating—alone or even in company" [11.42].

Arjuna's vision of Kṛṣṇa's cosmic form jolts him out of confident complacency. Recall Arjuna's opening request: ". . . O Supreme Lord, I want to see Your lordly form" [11.3]. Here Arjuna trusts in his intimate friendship with Kṛṣṇa.

Consider the somewhat common example of famous, rich, powerful people who choose to live where neighbors treat them simply as neighbors, not knowing or caring about the celebrity's celebrity. We know that famous, rich, powerful people have trouble finding true friends who love them for who they are, not for what they possess. Imagine, then, the situation of the supreme celebrity: God.

Thus Kṛṣṇa tells Arjuna: "I speak this spiritual science to you for you are My devoted friend" [4.3]. We know from *Mahābhārata* that Arjuna and his four brothers devoted their lives to Kṛṣṇa with great love; and Kṛṣṇa lived with them as if He were a human prince.

Such unassuming behavior on God's part can sometimes lead even the devoted to take the Lord for granted. Arjuna recognizes this after seeing the Lord's overwhelming cosmic form and apologizes [11.41–42]. He begs to again see the form of Kṛṣṇa that he knows and loves. After all, the cosmic form, for all its unbearable majesty, is hardly loveable. Kṛṣṇa complies and Arjuna sees Kṛṣṇa with new and chastened eyes.

Why did Arjuna ask to see the cosmic form at all? Arjuna tells Kṛṣṇa: "I want to see You, O Supreme Lord, as You described Yourself in Your lordly form" [11.3]. In other words, although Kṛṣṇa had mentioned many times that He is God Who rules all, Arjuna did not actually *see* these powers in His divine but modest friend. Essentially, Arjuna tells Kṛṣṇa: "You say You are God. Show me."

Kṛṣṇa replies: "Behold My hundreds and thousands of forms . . ." [11.5], "behold the entire universe here in one place, in My body" [11.7]. But Arjuna cannot see this cosmic revelation with his ordinary eyes, so Kṛṣṇa gives him *divine vision* [11.8]. Arjuna then beholds Kṛṣṇa's cosmic form, which shines like a thousand suns rising at once in the sky [11.12]. Arjuna sees the entire universe, with all its separate forms and divisions, within the body of the God of gods [11.13]. Astonished, hairs standing up, he bows to God, folds his hands and tells the Lord what he sees.

But then, he speaks of something new and dangerous: ". . . I see your mouth of blazing fire, burning the cosmos with splendor . . . Beholding this Your wondrous, fierce form, the three worlds tremble" [11.19–20]. Arjuna even sees frightened gods and great sages entering this flaring cosmic form, praying for their wellbeing [11.21]. The worlds tremble in fear [11.23].

This vision shakes Arjuna to the core of his being and he finds no peace [11.24]. Significantly, at this terrifying juncture, Arjuna, for the first time in the *Gītā*, addresses the Lord not as Kṛṣṇa, but rather with the more formal name *Viṣṇu* [11.24]. Arjuna then tells that the cosmic form is manifesting dreadful, gaping fangs. Completely disoriented, Arjuna finds no shelter and begs the Lord for mercy [11.25].

The battle warriors fly into the cosmic form's devouring mouths [11.26–27] like rivers rushing to the sea or moths rushing into fire [11.28–29]. The cosmic form starts to devour all the worlds. Again, calling the Lord *Viṣṇu* [11.30], Arjuna no longer knows Who or What he is seeing. He cries out: "Who are You, so fierce of form"? He then bows to Kṛṣṇa for the first time in *Bhagavad-gītā* [11.31].

The Lord replies: "Time I am, destroyer of worlds, expanded to withdraw the worlds" [11.32]. Kṛṣṇa—for it *is* Kṛṣṇa—then exhorts Arjuna to arise, attain glory and defeat the enemies. For as Kṛṣṇa declares: "I have already slain the enemies; [now] you just be the instrument" [11.33].

Hands folded, shaking, repeatedly bowing, voice choked, terrified—Arjuna offers prayers to God [11.35–46]. In these prayers he acknowledges that he took Kṛṣṇa for granted and prays: "O God, like father to son, friend to friend, lover to lover, be lenient to me" [11.44]!

Arjuna now prays to see not the Lord's cosmic, but rather His personal form. On his way back to stable, peaceful consciousness, he first asks to see Kṛṣṇa's renowned and majestic four-armed form as Viṣṇu [11.46]. After assuring Arjuna that only he has seen such extraordinary forms of the Lord, Kṛṣṇa again reveals His "sublime, humanlike form" as Arjuna's friend [11.50–51]. Seeing *this* form, Arjuna says: "Now I am restored, rational, natural" [11.51].

Kṛṣṇa assures Arjuna that only by exclusive devotion, and not by scriptural study, austerity, charity or ritual offering, can one see Kṛṣṇa as He *really* is [11.52–55]. And here the chapter ends.

We can draw several critical conclusions from this chapter. First, this chapter powerfully reaffirms monotheism. As Kṛṣṇa begins to reveal His cosmic form, He tells Arjuna to behold the gods within Him [11.6]. And when Arjuna receives the divine vision needed to see this form, his first statement is that he sees the gods inside God's cosmic body, including even Brahmā, the supreme creator god [11.15].

When the cosmic vision turns fearful, Arjuna states that the three worlds, *including* the highest realm of the gods, tremble in fear [11.20]. Hosts of terrified gods and great sages "enter You," praying for their own wellbeing [11.21]. These astonished gods all gaze upon Kṛṣṇa's cosmic form [11.22]. Arjuna declares that God surpasses even Brahmā, "the first maker" [11.37].

Careful scrutiny of this chapter suggests that Kṛṣṇa's cosmic form is *not* His full revelation of Himself, but rather the opposite: a very partial view of God. Apart from terror and confusion, we have no real relationship with the cosmic form. It doesn't really do anything except display infinite splendor and devour the cosmos.

Kṛṣṇa states that He is a kind-hearted friend to all beings [5.29], that He reciprocates His devotees' love [9.29], that to know Him as the Supreme Person is to know everything [15.19], and that He personally uplifts those devoted to Him [12.2]. The cosmic form offers nothing of this intimacy. God's love for us all, His eagerness to help us, is grimly absent in the cosmic form.

In fact, when Arjuna directly asks who the cosmic form is [11.31], He replies, "Time I am, destroyer of worlds" [11.32]. By comparison, Kṛṣṇa states in the previous chapter: "I am death that takes away everything *and* the coming forth of all that will be" [10.34]. The cosmic form wields only half of this tandem of powers. Kṛṣṇa declares: "I am the source of all; from Me all proceeds" [10.8]. The cosmic form contains and consumes the cosmos, but does not appear to create it.

Kṛṣṇa inspires Arjuna's love and devotion. The cosmic form terrifies the whole universe [11.20, 23] as well as Arjuna [11.24, 45], until it literally scares him out of his wits [11.24–25]. Only the return of Kṛṣṇa's original human-like form restores Arjuna to his own true nature, reviving his reason. Thus souls, represented by Arjuna, realize themselves fully in relation to Kṛṣṇa, not the cosmic form [11.51]. The soul is part of Kṛṣṇa [15.7], and achieves self-realization in relation to Kṛṣṇa. This points to Kṛṣṇa as God's full manifestation, not the brief show of God's omnipotence as all-devouring, implacable Time. Indeed throughout the *Mahā-bhārata* Arjuna often yearns to see Kṛṣṇa; but apart from his one request in *Bhagavad-gītā*, he shows no particular interest in seeing the cosmic form.

Nonetheless, the cosmic form does serve an essential purpose: it prevents Arjuna (and us) from taking Kṛṣṇa for granted, though this epiphany seems to have escaped many *Gītā* commentators. Still the cosmic form does chasten and illumine the devoted reader.

Elsewhere in the *Mahā-bhārata* [5.129] Kṛṣṇa displays an abridged version of His cosmic form. There too He awards divine vision to those fortunate to see it.

Next I will explain the *Gītā*'s concept of *buddhi*, spiritual intelligence or reason, which, Kṛṣṇa tells us, is essential for success on all spiritual paths. After this preface, we will then consider the specific spiritual paths that lead to liberation: *karma-yoga* (action-*yoga*), *jñāna-yoga* (knowledge-*yoga*), *dhyāna-yoga* (meditation-*yoga*) and *bhakti-yoga* (devotion-*yoga*).

PART VII
Yoga

The Power of Reason (*Buddhi*)

The word *buddhi* indicates intelligence, reason or judgment. It is the power to discern where to enter and where to exit, what to do and what not to do, in pursuit of our rational self-interest. *Buddhi* tells us what is benign and what is malign, what liberates and what enslaves. *Buddhi* makes these crucial distinctions [18.30].

Above the fickle mind that *likes* and *dislikes*, accepts and rejects, with subjective caprice, there is cool, calm, objective *buddhi*—the voice of reason. Standing next to soul in the scale of powers [3.42], *buddhi* is reason that reasons to what is beyond itself: eternal soul [3.43].

Indeed when we are drawn to spirituality in this life, we reconnect with the *buddhi*, spiritual understanding, of our past life. Thus we again strive for final perfection [6.43]. And with pure *buddhi*, we qualify for spiritual existence [18.51–53].

Some people claim, in the name of scripture, that there is nothing more to life than trading piety for material rewards [2.42–43]. But *yoga* as disciplined spiritual life is possible only when *buddhi* turns a deaf ear to material attachment, and to religious texts that promote pious materialism [2.52–53]. Thus in our battle against attachment and illusion our last line of defense is *buddhi*. If we lose our reason, the soul is surely lost in ignorance [2.63]. But in a life of joyful grace (*prasāda*) we vanquish our troubles, and *buddhi* stands firm [2.65]. This results from serious spiritual practice [2.66].

In this difficult world, Kṛṣṇa tells us to "seek shelter in *buddhi*" [2.49]: clear reason that tells us not to selfishly covet action's fruits. Indeed scientific findings indicate that people derive more pleasure by spending money on others rather than themselves. To renounce self-centeredness is not to renounce pleasure, but rather to find genuine pleasure in the devoted life. Virtuous happiness comes when *buddhi* finds serenity in real self [18.37]. *Buddhi* embraces the ultimate joy of self-realization, beyond the mundane senses [6.21]. Thus, with determined *buddhi*, one should gradually withdraw the mind from illusory objects and fix it in true self [6.25]. With pure *buddhi*, we see how to act without incurring *karma* [4.18]; with steady *buddhi*, we know and achieve the Absolute [5.20]; and with *equal-buddhi*, we see all beings equally as eternal souls, regardless of their body type or material condition [6.9]. This *equal-buddhi* helps us to attain Kṛṣṇa [12.4].

But lust can infect our reason and cover awareness [3.39]. Modes of passion and darkness corrupt *buddhi* [18.31–32]. In passion, *buddhi* inexactly measures what is and is not moral, what is and is not duty. In darkness, *buddhi* gets all matters backwards, taking the immoral to be moral [18.32].

But when *buddhi* detaches from all material things, one gives up mundane life and attains perfection beyond *karma* [18.49]. We need *buddhi* to free ourselves from *karma*'s bonds [2.39, 2.50], whether we tread the path of knowledge-*yoga* (*jñāna-yoga*) or action-*yoga* (*karma-yoga*).

Resolute reason guides us with laser focus; but when resolve weakens, reason scatters in endless directions [2.41]. Those who cling to mundane pleasure and power cannot focus *buddhi* on the spiritual path [2.44]; they fret over innumerable problems instead of pursuing a spiritual state that resolves them all.

What then inspires and empowers resolute reason (*buddhi*) to give up endless worries and solely focus on the spiritual path? It is none other than Kṛṣṇa, who repeatedly assures that He will personally take care of us *if* we take His instructions seriously.

Kṛṣṇa comes to this world to rescue the righteous from their troubles [4.8]. If we can grasp that He is the kind-hearted friend of all beings, we will find the peace that eludes us [5.29]. He personally brings prosperity and security to those devoted to Him [9.22]. He is our shelter (*śaraṇam*) and true friend [9.18], urging us to come to Him alone for shelter (*śaraṇam*) from all troubles, assuring us that we will thus find highest peace and everlasting abode, and that He will free us from all transgressions [18.62, 18.66].

Again using the same word for shelter, Kṛṣṇa tells the soul: "Seek shelter (*śaraṇam*) in *buddhi*" [2.49]. Thus, to seek shelter in *buddhi* is to embrace the pure reason that guides us to devote ourselves to God.

Grasping this spiritual logic, our intelligence stops agonizing over the inevitable problems of this world, be they financial, social, psychological, political, historical or whatever, and eagerly accepts Kṛṣṇa's offer of shelter, sustenance and eternal abode. Indeed, Kṛṣṇa states near the *Gītā*'s end that one should rely on *buddhi* and thus dedicate all one's actions to Kṛṣṇa, taking Him as supreme and always thinking of Him [18.57]. Again, the specific *buddhi* that one relies on here is pure reason absorbed in God. After all, one who finally attains knowledge after many births realizes that Kṛṣṇa is everything [7.19].

Thus the *Gītā* presents full devotion to Kṛṣṇa as a supremely rational act, the fruit of pure reason, *buddhi*. Souls do not come to Kṛṣṇa by rejecting reason. To the contrary, Kṛṣṇa states that He personally gives *buddhi-yoga* to the constantly devoted, who then come to Him by that practice of pure reason [10.10]. Indeed, the proof of pure *buddhi* is that one sees Kṛṣṇa as the Supreme

Person beyond all other persons, knowing that there is no higher understanding or scriptural truth [15.20].

Conversely, those who lack *buddhi* think that Kṛṣṇa is originally and ultimately impersonal, and that He takes on personal form for some purpose. Lacking *buddhi* (spiritual reason), they do not understand Kṛṣṇa's higher personal nature [7.24].

Worse still, the irrational, those with "paltry *buddhi*," believe there is no God in the universe, no Truth or foundation [16.8–9]. Similarly, those with "unformed *buddhi*" believe themselves the sole authors of their actions, heedless of environmental and providential factors [18.16].

We attain pure reason, *buddhi*, by devoting our reasoning to Kṛṣṇa. We do that by taking *Bhagavad-gītā* seriously. Kṛṣṇa tells us to offer our *buddhi* to Him [8.7, 12.14][1] and to *fix* our *buddhi* in Him [12.8].

Moreover, Kṛṣṇa Himself is the *buddhi* of those who possess it [7.10], since He lives in our heart and gives us knowledge [15.15] if we desire it.

Bhagavad-gītā presents its clearest and most succinct notion of a spiritual science in the term *buddhi-yoga*. The webpage *Oxford Dictionaries* defines science as "the intellectual and practical activity encompassing the systematic study of the . . . physical and natural world through observation and experiment."[2] Putting aside the question-begging presumption that one can *only* systematically study "the physical and natural world," we here focus on the "intellectual and practical" dimen-

---

[1] In these two verses, Kṛṣṇa uses the term *arpita*, "offered," a form of the term used for "offering" in 4.24, when Kṛṣṇa describes the offering to *brahman*, *brahma-arpaṇam*. *Arpaṇam* is a neuter noun, and *arpita* is a past passive participle. Thus having offered, *arpita*, one's God-given reason [7.4] back to God, one performs an essential type of *yajña*.

[2] http://www.oxforddictionaries.com/definition/english/science.

sions of such study. *Buddhi* indicates intelligence or reason and *yoga* indicates practice. It is the term *buddhi-yoga* that points to a spiritual science.

Thus Kṛṣṇa claims to give a rational understanding (*buddhi*) of the soul in both theory and practice [2.39]. This *buddhi-yoga* is far superior to ordinary action [2.50]; Kṛṣṇa bestows it on those always devoted to Him [10.10]. By depending on *buddhi-yoga*, one is able to always fix the mind on Kṛṣṇa [18.57].

Let us summarize the essential and general traits of *yoga*, the spiritual path, and then explore the distinct traits of the chief *yoga* paths.

Three times in the *Gītā*, Kṛṣṇa says of a person in a specific state of consciousness: "*That* is a *yogī*." Each of these verses describes a distinct qualification that enables a true *yogī* to see self, God and other souls. Thus:

1. A *yogī* or spiritual practitioner finds joy, pleasure and light within—in the true self [5.24].
2. A *yogī* stands in unity and sees Kṛṣṇa in all beings, thus existing in all circumstances in Kṛṣṇa [6.31].
3. A *yogī*, by comparing self to others, sees equally everywhere, in joy and sorrow [6.32].

Once again, *buddhi*, spiritual reason or discernment, helps a *yogī* to properly see self, God and other souls.

A *yogī* is higher than one pursing either knowledge (*jñānī*) or action (*karmī*) [6.46]. But what makes action-*yoga* (*karma-yoga*) better than mere action? What makes knowledge-*yoga* (*jñāna-yoga*) better than mere knowledge? Or one could ask: What turns action into action-*yoga*? What turns knowledge into knowledge-*yoga*? To answer these questions, we will first examine these two famous *yoga* paths—and then consider that which stands above both.

Spiritual Practice (*Yoga*)

It is often noted that the word *yoga* comes from the Sanskrit root *yuj*, meaning, in the sense relevant here: "to join, link, connect," "to prepare, make ready," "to use or engage," "to meditate on and unite with God."[3]

Thus, without significant semantic stretching, we can say that *yoga*—both in the Sanskrit dictionary and in *Bhagavad-gītā*—primarily refers to a spiritual practice in which one readies the soul to unite with God.

The *Gītā* knows and respects the fact that people are different, and so presents alternative *yoga* paths. True to its name, *karma-yoga* (action-*yoga*) attracts active people who, like most of us, wish to act dynamically but spiritually in the world,[4] whereas *jñāna-yoga* (knowledge-*yoga*) suits those inclined to approach Truth intellectually, philosophically [3.3].

Kṛṣṇa declares that the action and knowledge paths are ultimately one, for either, practiced well, bestows the benefit of both [5.4–5]: a diligent, devoted *karma-yogī* sees the soul as much as does the spiritual philosopher [13.25]; and a successful *jñāna-yogī* must apply knowledge in the world [3.25]. Later in the *Gītā*, Kṛṣṇa also teaches *dhyāna-yoga* (meditation-*yoga*), designed for the mystic meditator [13.25, 18.53, etc.].

While Kṛṣṇa does not rank *karma-yoga*, *jñāna-yoga* and *dhyāna-yoga*, He *does* clearly place *bhakti-yoga*, the *yoga* of pure love, above all these others [6.47, 12.1–2].

---

[3] The same root *yuj*, which produces the word *yoga*, also gives us a word found forty-six times in the *Gītā*: *yukta*, a past passive participle. Thus while *yoga* means "to link," *yukta* means "linked"; and while *yoga* means "to engage," *yukta* means "engaged." As such, "one who is *yukta* is said to be a *yogī*" [6.8].

[4] In the *Gītā* the words *yoga* and *yogī* sometimes mean *karma-yoga* and *karma-yogī* [2.39, 3.3, 5.4–5, etc.], this being by far the largest *yoga* group, since most people choose to work in the world.

Each of these *yoga* paths will be discussed separately, but first I will explain the general characteristics of all such paths.

Equality (*Samatvam*)

Kṛṣṇa first defines *yoga* as *samatvam*, "equality" or "evenness" [2.48]—a stoic state of consciousness in which one staunchly stays aloof from mundane attraction and aversion.[5] This *equality* or *equanimity* is thus the opposite of, and the antidote for, *dvandva*, dualities such as joy and sorrow, victory and defeat, gain and loss, fame and infamy. In the above section on *karma* I listed these dualities, saying that trapped in dualities and their extremes of joy and sorrow, we love and hate material objects, forgetting that our real self exists beyond all material objects.

Kṛṣṇa explains that a true *yogī* can tolerate mundane dualities of pleasing and displeasing objects and situations because they are all *outside*—i.e., extrinsic to, and ultimately separate from, the pure soul. The *yogī* focuses *within*.

Kṛṣṇa uses this language of *outside* and *inside* to describe, respectively, the physical world, which the soul perceives through material bodily senses, and inner spiritual reality, which the soul perceives directly—i.e., not through the medium of a physical body. For example, a soul detaches from *external contacts* (the physical body with the physical world) by discovering the unperishing pleasure *within* the self [5.21]. Thus, placing *outside contacts outside* (where they belong), one practices *yoga* [5.28].

Kṛṣṇa often indicates inner consciousness with the word *ātmani*, "within the soul/self," as in these examples:

---

[5] Kṛṣṇa uses the word *samatvam* or *sama* ("even, equal") in this sense in many verses: 2.15, 2.38, 4.22, 5.18, 6.8–9, 12.14, 12.18, 13.10, 14.24. He also uses a close synonym, *tulya*, in the same sense of being equal in the face of material dualities: 12.19, 14.24–25.

When one is satisfied *in self alone*, one's wisdom is fixed [2.55].

One who delights *in self alone*, content *in self*, satisfied *in self alone*, has no worldly duty [3.17].

When awareness stands *in self alone*, one is actually linked in *yoga* [6.18].

Wherever the mind wanders, one must bring it back under control *in self alone* [6.26].

Kṛṣṇa also indicates *inner* awareness with the word *antar* (inner or within), as in these examples:

"*That* is a *yogī* who, with *inner* joy, *inner* delight and real *inner* light, lives as Brahman and attains *nirvāṇa* in Brahman" [5.24].

The most advanced *yogī* goes to Me with *inner* self [6.47].

Strikingly, *yogīs* see not only *within* themselves, but also *within* all of nature. We should not cling to external nature, but we should see God and other souls *within* nature. Thus:

A linked *yogī* sees the soul in all beings [6.29].

One who sees Kṛṣṇa within all and all within Kṛṣṇa is never lost to Kṛṣṇa, nor is Kṛṣṇa ever lost to that person [6.30].

A *yogī*, abiding in unity, worships Kṛṣṇa in all beings [6.31].

One who sees the Supreme Lord abiding *equally* in all beings, actually sees [13.28].

Seeing the Lord *equally* everywhere, one does not harm oneself; then one travels on the highest path [13.29].

That is the highest *yogī* who, by comparison with self, sees *equally* everywhere, in joy or sorrow [6.32].

Indeed that pure *yogī* becomes "a self, being the self of all beings" [5.7].[6]

---

[6] "Being the self of all beings" indicates full spiritual empathy.

Thus the best *yogī*—a purified soul with complete, deep, universal empathy—feels for every soul *as if being* that soul. Such a *yogī* sees each soul equally within Kṛṣṇa and Kṛṣṇa equally within each soul.

Kṛṣṇa is the ultimate basis of *samatvam*, equality, also called *ekatvam*, unity or oneness. All souls are part of Him [15.7], and are one with each other in Him. We have already discussed in what sense Kṛṣṇa is everything [7.19]: He is all, for He encompasses all [11.40], for He is the source of all [7.4–5, 10.8].

Kṛṣṇa Himself sets the example of equal vision, for He is equal to all beings [9.29]. Sincere souls, including *yogīs*, follow Kṛṣṇa's example [3.21–23, 4.14]. Indeed one who knows in truth Kṛṣṇa's vast power and *yoga* also engages in unwavering *yoga* [10.7], for everything flows from Kṛṣṇa [10.8]—including *yoga*. As Kṛṣṇa sends rain to the farmer [3.14–15, 9.19], He sends *yoga* to the *yogī*. The *Gītā* itself is *yoga* [4.1–3].

Thus, as Arjuna and Sañjaya both declare, Kṛṣṇa is the Lord of *yoga* [11.4, 18.75–78], indeed the Great Lord of *yoga* [11.9]. By His ruling *yoga* Kṛṣṇa maintains and governs all beings [9.5, 11.8], by His bewildering *yoga* power (*yoga-māyā*) He conceals Himself [7.25], and by His personal *yoga* power He reveals Himself [11.47].

No one is equal to or greater than Kṛṣṇa [11.43], and so, as the natural leader of creation, Kṛṣṇa establishes the unity and spiritual equality of all that He creates. Kṛṣṇa declares that *yoga is equality* [2.48] and that the highest *yogī* sees equally everywhere [6.32]: within oneself, within others and within all of nature. Thus a material world of dead matter and confused souls magically springs to life when we see Kṛṣṇa everywhere, everything in Kṛṣṇa, and the true spiritual nature of all life.

In that liberating state, *buddhi* (reason) is everywhere detached and free [18.49]. One is then *equal* in external joy and sorrow, heat and cold [2.16, 12.18]. Indeed one *makes* joy and sorrow the same [2.38]. For one thus standing in self, the dualities collapse. One sees equally sorrow and joy, earth and gold, the pleasing and displeasing, censure and praise, honor and dishonor. In that state of *yoga-equality*, one transcends nature's modes. In other words, one is liberated [14.24–25].

Elsewhere Kṛṣṇa repeats that a *yogī* (literally, a "*linker*") is considered linked upon seeing earth, stone and gold *equally* [6.8]. Similarly, success and failure become *equal* [2.48]; indeed, one *makes* them *equal* [4.22].

On the social front, a *yogī* with equal-*buddhi* sees the ultimate spiritual equality of friends, foes, abstainers, mediators, the odious, the kindred and even saints and sinners, and thus surpasses one who merely sees physical objects as equal. Kṛṣṇa adds that those with equal-*buddhi* devote themselves to the welfare of *all beings everywhere* and come to Kṛṣṇa [12.4]. In other words, equal vision is not merely passive indifferent awareness, but rather the powerful vision that every living thing is spiritually equal to ourselves, and thus part of a single divine family. With this vision, one can fulfill the celebrated command to "love your neighbor as you love yourself," with the sublime addition that *all living beings*—not just humans—are our neighbors. It hardly needs saying that such a vision of life would bring spectacular environmental benefits.

Samatvam, spiritual equality, requires and inspires true compassion, beyond the attachment and hatred that usually infect political and social causes. Such causes, based on duality, sew the seed of future hostility even as they address present conflict.

Thus Kṛṣṇa describes those most dear to Him as follows: they do not hate any being; they are friendly and especially kind to all beings; they have no sense of ego or possessiveness; they are equal in joy and sorrow; and they are forgiving [12.13]. Further, they are equal to foe and friend, equal in honor and dishonor, cold and heat, joy and sorrow, slander and praise—for they are ever-satisfied *yogīs* [12.18–19].

Here "equal to foe and friend" does not mean that a *yogī* is helplessly and hopelessly impractical. Remember that Kṛṣṇa is teaching this to Arjuna, an on-duty warrior who Kṛṣṇa instructs to fight. The equality Kṛṣṇa speaks of is a spiritual state of mind that empowers even a warrior to act in the best possible way. Thus, after the Battle of Kuru-kṣetra, Arjuna and his brothers ruled the world with kindness towards all—even former enemies.

Speaking of *all*, the wise extend their equal vision and kindness to all life, since every living being is part of God [15.7]. Thus the wise see with *equal vision* both high- and low-class persons as well as cows, elephants and dogs [5.18]. It is the nature of *brahman* (spirit) to be equal to all; thus one whose mind stands in equality stands in *brahman* [5.19]. Having attained *brahman* existence (pure spiritual life), one is equal to all beings and attains highest love for God [18.54].

Kṛṣṇa makes clear that an advanced *yogī* has equal vision *everywhere* [6.29], equal intelligence *everywhere* [12.4]. Hearing of this ambitious cognitive project, Arjuna protests that it is too difficult to achieve, for the mind is fickle and unstable [6.33-34]. Kṛṣṇa, however, assures him that by sincere spiritual practice and detachment one can indeed attain equality [6.35].

Arjuna then asks about the fate of a *yogī* who tries and fails [3.36–38]. Kṛṣṇa's reply inspires and comforts the spiritual practitioner: no one who does good in this world meets a bad fate at the end. The unsuccessful *yogī* takes birth in a higher world, living a blessed life for long celestial years, and then takes a privileged birth on earth; or the fallen *yogī* is directly reborn on earth in a family of wise spiritualists, where spiritual awareness and practice are quickly revived and perfection is achieved at last [6.40–45].

As stated, this perfection entails equal vision, and Kṛṣṇa assures us that we can achieve equal vision by spiritual practice, which always entails the attainment of *brahman* existence. The *yogī*, linked in *brahma-yoga*, enjoys unperishing pleasure [5.21]; indeed, the highest pleasure comes to a *yogī* who lives as *brahman* [6.27]. Kṛṣṇa teaches that *yoga* is practiced to purify self [5.11, 6.12, 6.45] and that the wise *yogī* attains *brahman*, freedom from *karma*, without delay [5.7]. Yet He also teaches that the act of *yajña*, offering, is the only path to freedom from *karma* [3.9]. *Yajña*, not *yoga*, transforms offering and offerer, as well as oblation, fire and reward, into *brahman* [4.24]. What then is the relationship between *yoga* and *yajña*?

Renunciation (*Sannyāsa*)

At the start of Chapter Six, Kṛṣṇa brings *yoga* and *yajña*[7] together in an interesting way. Having taught that "*yoga* is equality" [2.48], Kṛṣṇa now states that "*yoga* is renunciation, for no one becomes a *yogī* who does not renounce selfish will" [6.2].[8]

Yet one who is a true renouncer, and thus a true *yogī*, performs necessary duties, whereas "the fireless is no *yogī*" [6.1]. Fire here, of course, refers to sacred fire[9] (literal or symbolic), which receives and consumes one's offering [4.25-30]. The point is clear: a *yogī* must perform prescribed duties, and prominent among those duties is *yajña*. No *yajña*, no *yoga*.

To understand this crucial connection between spiritual practice (*yoga*), renunciation and offering, we must closely look at what Kṛṣṇa means when He speaks of renouncing. Renunciation is a central topic in *Bhagavad-gītā* for two reasons: 1) Arjuna wants to renounce the battle, and Kṛṣṇa insists that Arjuna misunderstands renunciation; and, 2) Kṛṣṇa teaches

---

[7] *Yajña* denotes an offering or sacrifice to God or His representatives.

[8] The word *saṅkalpa* can mean *will* or *volition* in general, but Kṛṣṇa always uses the term to mean a *selfish* will that one must give up in order to advance spiritually [4.19, 6.2, 6.4, 6.24].

[9] Fire is *agni*, cognate with Latin *ignis* (fire) and English *ignite*.

liberation, and one must properly renounce this world to attain liberation.

Kṛṣṇa mainly uses two words to indicate *renunciation*: *tyāga* and *sannyāsa*.[10] A dramatic difference between these synonyms highlights the *Gītā*'s teaching on renunciation.

The word *tyāga* in various forms[11] unequivocally means abandoning, renouncing or forsaking something. Thus Kṛṣṇa uses this word to describe: the soul giving up the material body at death [4.9, 8.6, 8.13], rejecting all possessiveness [4.21], giving up all desires born of selfish will [6.24], rejecting lust, anger and greed [16.21], etc.

Kṛṣṇa also defines *tyāga* to mean giving up the fruit of all actions [18.2], and often uses the word in this sense,[12] as well as in the sense of giving up attachment to the fruit of actions.[13]

But as stated at 6.1, one *must not* give up prescribed duties. Thus sacrifice, charity and austerity are not to be given up (*na tyājyam*); they must be performed [18.5]. Also, one must not give up (*na tyajet*) one's natural work in life [18.48]. Indeed it is impossible for an embodied soul to give up (*tyaktum*) actions entirely. A renouncer (*tyāgī*) is one who renounces action's fruit [18.11], etc.

Kṛṣṇa never states that *tyāga*, mere rejecting, is *yoga*. Rather *yoga* is *sannyāsa*, a word meaning not merely to renounce things, but also to positively entrust or commit them to the proper place or person.

---

[10] Kṛṣṇa also twice uses forms of the verb *hā* (to give up): once to warn Arjuna that he will give up duty and fame if he doesn't fight [2.33]; and once to state that the *Gītā* teaches one to give up *karma*-bondage [2.39].

[11] As a noun (*tyāga*), indeclinable participle (*tyaktvā*, and once, *parityajya*), agent noun (*tyāgī* or *parityāgī*), present participle (*tyajan*), past passive participle (*tyakta*), infinitive (*tyaktum*), and gerundive (*tyājya*).

[12] 2.51, 4.20, 5.12, 12.11–12, 18.6, 18.9–11.

[13] 2.48, 4.20, 5.10–11, 18.6, 18.9–10.

The word *sannyāsa* consists of three semantic elements: *sam-ni-āsa*, meaning to properly or completely (*sam*) place something (*āsa*) down or within (*ni*). Thus *sannyāsa* can mean to place *down* (and thus renounce) or to place *within* (and thus entrust or commit something to another person).

The *Gītā* clearly uses the word *sannyāsa* in both ways. In the sense of giving up something, Kṛṣṇa uses the word when stating that no one can be a *yogī* who does not *give up* selfish desire [6.2], that an advanced *yogī gives up* all selfish desire [6.4], that one who *gives up* duality, and who does not hate or hanker, is to be known as a steady renouncer [5.3], and that the learned say that renunciation is *giving up* selfish actions [18.2].

However, Kṛṣṇa emphasizes that merely giving up the mundane will not liberate one without a positive spiritual agenda. Thus, one does not achieve perfection by mere renunciation [3.4], action-*yoga* (*karma-yoga*) is better than renouncing action [5.2], renunciation is difficult to attain without positive spiritual practice (*yoga*) [5.6], a renouncer (*sannyāsī*) must execute prescribed duties [6.1], and renunciation of prescribed duty is inappropriate [18.7].

Kṛṣṇa uses the word *sannyāsa*[14] to show that a *yogī* renounces not only in the negative sense of rejecting, but also in the positive sense of putting things where they belong, entrusting or committing them to God. In the following examples, I translate the verb *sannyasya* as *commits*:

Aware of higher self, one *commits* all actions to Kṛṣṇa [3.30].

With fully focused *yoga*, one *commits* all actions to Kṛṣṇa [12.6].

With awareness and devotion, one *commits* all actions to Kṛṣṇa [18.57].

---

[14] Kṛṣṇa uses the word variously as a noun (*sannyāsa*), indeclinable participle (*sannyasya*), agent-noun (*sannyāsi*), and past passive participle (*sannyasta*).

Recall that in this world we all must act at every moment [3.5] and the only action that frees us from *karma*-bondage is *yajña*, offering [3.9]. *Yoga* in its highest sense of spiritual practice is certainly an activity, and thus *yoga* can liberate us *only when performed as an offering*. Thus Kṛṣṇa states that without positive spiritual practice (*yoga*) mere renunciation leads to unhappiness, whereas a sage engaged in *yoga* quickly attains the Absolute [5.6].

Thus, after explaining how a spiritual offering spiritualizes the offered article and the offerer [4.24], Kṛṣṇa at once describes how *yogīs* offer their various *yoga* practices, including breathing exercises, meditation and sacred study, to the Divine [4.25-29]. Kṛṣṇa concludes at 4.30: "All these [*yogīs*] do indeed know sacrifice; sacrifice removes their sins. Eating the nectar-remnant of sacrifice, they go to eternal Brahman."

Clearly *yoga* techniques alone—breathing, focusing, etc.—do not dispel *karma*; for without a devoted offering, they are merely physical and mental acts. One forges a link (*yoga*) to the Absolute through *yajña*, offering one's *yoga* actions to God.

Kṛṣṇa then reaffirms what He said at 3.9: neither this world nor any other is for those who make no offering [4.31] or who doubt these facts [4.40]. Thus *yoga* liberates us when we offer our spiritual practice to God: *yoga* supplies technique and discipline and *yajña* gives the intention and devotion that inspire and spiritualize the discipline—as indicated by the term *yoga-yajña*, the offering of *yoga* [4.28]. It is *yajña* that transforms matter to spirit [4.24, 9.16] and dissolves *karma* [3.9, 4.23]. In the list of acts that one may never give up—i.e., offering, charity and austerity [18.5]—*yoga* is notably absent.

Yajña destroys our *kalmaṣa* (impurity) [4.30], and the purified *yogī* sees God and souls everywhere with *yoga*'s sublime equal vision. Indeed the bliss of *yoga* comes to a *yogi* whose *kalmaṣa* (impurity) is thus destroyed [6.28-32]. One who does not turn the cosmic wheel of receiving and offering back [3.16], and who is thus a thief, living in vain [3.12], can hardly be a spiritual *yogī*. All souls must offer; and one should offer one's *yoga* to Yogeśvara: *Yoga* Lord, Kṛṣṇa. Again, just as Kṛṣṇa sends rain to the farmer who performs *yajña* [3.14–15, 9.19], so He provides *yoga* for the devoted *yogī* [6.47, 10.7].

Finally, as mentioned, Kṛṣṇa describes His teaching, *Bhagavad-gītā*, as *yoga* [4.1–3], and at its end declares that one who studies this teaching honors the Lord through the offering of knowledge, *jñāna-yajña*. Again, *yoga* is an offering, in this case offering one's studies to Kṛṣṇa by studying His book.

Yoga surpasses mundane *yajña* [8.28], but spiritual *yajña* [4.24] is the framework of all spiritual paths. *Yoga* is a subset of *yajña* [4.28], but *yajña* is never said to be a type of *yoga*. *Yajña* is the *sine qua non*: the one *required* attitude and act for souls strapped to *karma*'s wheel and seeking freedom from birth and death. One should thus practice *yoga in a spirit of devoted offering*.

PART VIII
Karma-yoga (Action-*Yoga*)

Arjuna's Problem

In the final portion of this work, I will explain the *Gītā*'s various spiritual paths, beginning where Kṛṣṇa began—with *karma-yoga*. Early in the *Gītā*, Arjuna wrongly assumed *buddhi*, spiritual awareness, to be a passive state in which one withdraws from the world and does not act in it [3.1, 5.1]. His motive, of course, was to avoid his warrior's duty to fight. To correct Arjuna's misconceptions, Kṛṣṇa taught him the path of *karma-yoga*.

In the previous section I discussed the universal features of all spiritual paths, or *yoga*s, as taught in the *Gītā*. *Karma-yoga* entails these shared spiritual features: *samatvam* (equality), *sannyāsa* (giving up selfish will) and *yajña* (dedicating one's spiritual practice to God).

Like Arjuna long ago, today's entangled seekers often feel that they can live a spiritual life only by renouncing the world and secluding themselves in nature, a monastery or an ashrama.

But Kṛṣṇa teaches that we can achieve spiritual perfection within the world if we spiritualize our normal life and duties by way of *karma-yoga*. Thus he states that "simply by action [in the world], great kings like Janaka achieved full perfection" [3.20]. Indeed both the wise and the unwise act in this world, but the wise act with pure intent so as to guide the world by their example [3.20, 25].

Most people are not disciplined philosophers or reclusive mystics. Most work for a living, support a family and seek normal human pleasures. It is this *normal* life that *karma-yoga* spiritualizes by a simple means: offering the fruit of all we do to God. Let us look more closely at how *karma-yoga* works.

The Need for Action

Making his argument for *karma-yoga*, Kṛṣṇa first establishes that total inaction is not an option for a soul in this world. Playing on two central meanings of *karma*—action and the *law of karma* (as commonly known today)—Kṛṣṇa states that one does not get free of *karma* (action and reaction) simply by not undertaking *karma* (action). Nor does one achieve perfection simply by renunciation [3.4]. Why not? Because in this world no one can stop acting—not even for a moment [3.5]. Even meditation is an act, as is the *act* of renouncing. Thus total inaction is not an option. Even the wise act according to their nature. Beings follow their nature. What will repression do [3.33]?

So we all must act in this world. And because we seek that which pleases and avoid that which displeases, we act to secure action's fruits, both for ourselves and for those that are close. Thus we act for health, prosperity, fame, power, security, love, comfort, knowledge, bodily pleasure, etc. At the simplest level, we eat to please and nourish our body. And by clinging to action's fruits, we are bound to the *karma* cycle of birth and death.

Action as *Yoga* and *Yajña*

Kṛṣṇa tells us that since we must act, we have a right to act, but we are never entitled to the fruits of action [2.47], as we discussed in the section on *yajña*, offering. Briefly, just as the hand feeds itself by feeding the body, of which it is part, we nourish our existence by offering action's fruits to Kṛṣṇa, of Whom we are part [15.7]. Indeed Kṛṣṇa is the *source* of our existence and our ability to act. By this offering we establish a state of *yoga*, a divine link to our source, and we become *yukta*, linked. By acting selfishly and grasping the fruit of our work we become *a-yukta*, disconnected from our source, like a withering leaf detached from a tree; and thus we are bound by *karma*'s stringent laws [5.12].

Again, we are active by nature. If we try to stop the body from acting, the mind will still hypocritically focus on sense objects. Thus Kṛṣṇa emphasizes that "*karma-yoga* is better" since it spiritually engages the active senses [3.6–7] and "*karma-yoga* is better than giving up actions" [5.2].

Similarly, those who are real renouncers perform action as duty and offer to the Lord [6.1]. It is impossible for an embodied soul to entirely give up action; one who gives up the *fruit* of action is a true renouncer [18.11].

If we do not engage our nature in *karma-yoga*, our nature will act anyway, outside the safe boundaries of spiritual practice, and drag us back down to the material platform [18.60]—for nature will act.

Kṛṣṇa steadily assures Arjuna that he must act in this world, but that *karma-yoga* will spiritualize those actions; indeed *karma-yoga* enables one to see the self [13.25].

Thus *karma-yoga* transforms life itself into *yajña*, a spiritual offering to God, and is the only means to escape *karma*-bondage [3.9]. As we saw in the section on *yajña*, the act of offering action's fruit to God (*karma-yoga*) creates a spiritual link (*yoga*) that spiritualizes our actions [4.24], leading us to liberation.

Karma-yoga allows us to continue performing all our normal, decent activities, but as an offering, *yajña*, to God. Thus within *karma* (action) there is *akarma*, freedom from the bondage of material reactions [4.18]. *Karma-yoga*, a form of offering, spiritualizes our work in this world [4.24] because we offer its fruits to the Supreme. *Karma-yoga* enables us to achieve spiritual perfection by offering the fruits of our career (or *karma*, in that sense of the word) to God [18.45–46]. Otherwise, our deeds and career perpetuate *karma-bandha*,[1] "*karma-bondage*" [2.39, 3.9, 9.28], also called "*birth-bondage*" [2.51], since *karma* forces us to take repeated births.

But, in practice, what does it mean to offer our actions (or actions' fruits) to God, thereby transforming *karma* into *karma-yoga*?

Career as *Yoga*

The word *karma* has another important sense that gives a special meaning to *karma-yoga*. *Karma* often indicates one's natural vocation, duty or career. Since people maintain both themselves and their loved ones with the fruits of their careers, and since one's career tends to define one's primary role in and contribution to society, *karma-yoga* first of all seeks to spiritualize our vocation or career in life.

In Sanskrit, *sva* means *one's own*.[2] After many lives of *karma* we accumulate a specific worldly nature or state of being called *sva-bhāva*. This is not our eternal spiritual nature, but rather a temporary conditioned state in this world. Still, if we are to spiritualize our life, we must engage our present worldly nature in *karma-yoga*. Otherwise that nature will act materially and bind us to this world [18.60]. Thus from our condition within a body (our *sva-bhāva*) comes our personal duty, vocation or career (our *sva-karma*)—the fruits of which sustain us. Kṛṣṇa states that we are created to make offerings [3.10], and we make offerings from within our natural vocation. Offering the fruits

---

[1] Also called *karma-bandhana*, which means the same thing.

[2] *Sva* is cognate with Spanish *su*, Portuguese *seu/sua*, Italian *suo/sua*, French *son/sa*, etc. All these words indicate possession: "his, her, its, one's own."

of our career to God turns *karma* into *karma-yoga*. Throughout the *Gītā*, Kṛṣṇa requests us to offer all our actions to Him.[3] This does not mean that we blindly give away our possessions or neglect those who need us, but rather that we use our assets to help others in a spirit of devotion.

Traditional Vedic culture, with its pre-industrial agrarian economy, divided society into four primary vocations, also called *varṇas*. Kṛṣṇa declares that He personally created this four-*varṇa* system based not on birth, as in a hereditary caste system, but rather on each person's qualities and natural work [4.13].

In this modern age, each of us must locate ourselves within this system in order to find our natural vocation. Here is the four-*varṇa* system:

1. *Brāhmaṇas* are society's teachers, priests and spiritual guides; a *brāhmaṇa* is naturally peaceful, self-controlled, austere, clean, forgiving, honest, learned, wise and trusting in God [18.42].
2. *Kṣatriyas* are society's rulers and protectors; a *kṣatriya* is naturally heroic, strong, determined, clever, unwavering in battle, generous and a leader [18.43].
3. *Vaiśyas* are society's farmers and merchants, and are naturally inclined to those vocations [18.44].
4. *Śudras* are society's workers and artisans, and are naturally inclined to assist the other *varṇas* [18.44].

And it is our old friends, the above-discussed modes of goodness, passion and darkness that determine our nature, thus making the list of vocations a type of modal map. One who primarily lives in goodness manifests the *brāhmaṇa* qualities, whereas a passionate person finds a warrior's duties natural, and so on. Arjuna's nature binds him to his warrior duty and

---

[3] 3.30, 9.27, 12.6, 12.10, 18.56, 18.57.

will force him to perform it, whether he wishes to or not [18.60]. Thus if one does not accept one's natural duty in a spirit of *karma-yoga*, one's nature will force one to act outside the cultural and spiritual safety of that path [18.59]. Every duty in this world has some disadvantage, yet one incurs grave danger by rejecting one's duty [3.35, 18.47].

Here it should be noted that although we follow our nature, we still have free will. I will explain this in terms of the *Gītā*'s systematic philosophy, and then illustrate the basic ideas with a modern example.

Inaction in Action

In clear consciousness, we realize that soul simply witnesses the motions and acts of a material body that covers the soul as clothes cover the body [2.22]. Thus only a soul bewildered by egotism (*ahaṅkāra*) thinks "I am the doer." In reality, (bodily) actions are all being carried out by nature's modes [3.27]. One who knows these principles of modes and actions does not cling to actions, realizing that when a physical body acts in the physical world, "modes are acting in modes" [3.28]. Thus, one who sees oneself as the non-doer, truly sees [13.30]. Indeed, when the seer sees no other doer but the modes, and knows what is beyond the modes, the seer then achieves Kṛṣṇa's own pure spiritual state [14.19].

How are we to understand all this? Kṛṣṇa teaches that we have free will [18.63] and thus cause our own joy and sorrow by our choices [13.21]. Kṛṣṇa does not force us to do good or evil; nor does He force us to chase the fruits of our actions. Rather, our own mode-conditioned nature (*sva-bhāva*) is acting [5.14–15, 18.41].

This may seem confusing. At times Kṛṣṇa states that nature's modes perform actions and that we are not doers. Elsewhere Kṛṣṇa states that we are responsible for our actions and thus suffer and enjoy their consequences. Kṛṣṇa clarifies this paradox in a series of statements in Chapters Thirteen and Fifteen:

Nature is the reason for cause, effect and agency; soul causes the experience of joy and sorrow [13.21].

We are responsible for the body's acts because our free choices set matter in motion. The body responds to our will but action happens—only the body moves, not the pure soul.

Kṛṣṇa illustrates this point with an example: just as physical objects never affect the space that contains them, so the body does not truly taint or transform the soul [13.33]. Here is what this means: objects exist in space, yet a red cloth in space does not make that space red. Space contains a red object but does not mix with it because space is subtler than the objects it contains. Pure space has no color, shape or texture.

Similarly, soul is subtler than matter, being a superior energy [7.4–5]. Thus matter never actually touches the soul. Souls are never material, just as space is never red, smooth, heavy or light. Rather, because we believe we *are* the body, and cling to that identity, we feel that we enjoy and suffer the body's pleasures and pains. In fact, however, we are aloof from the body [13.33].

By choices and actions, we condition our body to be good, passionate or ignorant. When we encounter a body, house, city, music, art, work, friendship, love or whatever—anything with material modes that appeal to our own psychophysical modes—our body and mind yearn for that object.

Thus when our body and mind interact with other bodies and minds, or other worldly objects, modes are acting in and upon modes. In a higher sense, nothing else is going on. Knowing this, one does not cling to those modes [3.28]. To the extent that we falsely identify with our material body and mind—and its modes—we believe that we and other persons move when the body moves.

Similarly, one who knows true principles (*tattva-vit*) should think, "I do nothing at all." For even while performing basic bodily functions like seeing, hearing, touching, eating or breathing, in fact, "senses are acting in sense objects" [5.8–9]. And physical senses are not our eternal self. Again, we merely witness the body's acts.

Thus, though engaged in action, one who neither clings to action's fruit nor depends on material circumstances does nothing at all [4.20]. One who possesses *buddhi*, spiritual reason, sees inaction in action [4.18]: body acts while soul witnesses.

Now let us consider a modern example to illustrate this concept and how it relates to *karma-yoga*. Imagine you are driving a car at high speed and suddenly realize you are going in the wrong direction—or worse, heading for a collision. At high speed, you cannot instantly stop your car, but you *can* steer it into a safe lane while gradually braking.

Similarly, our body (the soul's vehicle) races through time with psychological and behavioral momentum accumulated over many lives. Thus in career, relationships and recreation we seek to enjoy the fruits of our actions. Even when we see that our true nature and pleasure is spiritual, our desires, needs and propensities have momentum from many lives. We cannot instantly stop them. Rather we must steer our actions into spiritual channels while putting a brake on mundane attachments. No matter how spiritual the soul may be, the body will act according to its modes [3.5, 3.28, 33].

Material modes and the duties they generate are hierarchal, with virtue and virtue-born *brāhmaṇa* work being highest. Kṛṣṇa emphasizes that *karma-yoga* is the great equalizer. All persons can achieve full spiritual perfection by worshipping, through the performance of duty, He from whom everything emanates and by whom all is pervaded [18.45–46]. Again, *yoga* is *samatvam*, equality. Everyone in every *varṇa* is equal if they perform *karma-yoga* seriously; and those who do so, see all souls as equal.

On the path of *karma-yoga*, we learn to offer action's fruits to God. As our spiritual pleasure grows, we outgrow our attachment to material pleasure. Our spiritual practice awakens our eternal nature, beyond the body, freeing us to fulfill our highest dreams and ideals. Otherwise, as noted earlier, our deeds and career perpetuate *karma-bandha*, "*karma*-bondage" [2.39, 3.9, 9.28], also described as *birth-bondage* [2.51].

Though we must act according to our nature, we do have a powerful choice to make. If we work selfishly and try to enjoy action's fruits, our work (*karma*) binds us in nature's mortal net. Yet that same *karma*, if offered to Kṛṣṇa, transforms into liberating *karma-yoga* [18.45–46]. This is the essence of *karma-yoga*. Outwardly, *karma* and *karma-yoga* may look like the same deed. But internally, intention and consciousness are dramatically different and produce opposite results. Kṛṣṇa personally shows how to act in this world without attachment, just to set a good example for others [3.21–24, 4.14, 9.7–9].

But what of intellectuals whose nature is to seek Truth in serious, disciplined study? What is their path?

PART IX
Jñāna-yoga (Knowledge-*Yoga*)

Knowledge as a Spiritual Path

Kṛṣṇa explains that *jñāna-yoga* (knowledge-*yoga*) is for the philosophical, whereas *karma-yoga* (action-*yoga*) is for those that are active in the world. Yet repeatedly Kṛṣṇa emphasizes that both paths are simply aspects of a single spiritual position or standing called *niṣṭhā*[1] [3.3]. Kṛṣṇa affirms the unity of these two *yogas*: "The childish, not the wise, claim that analysis and practice are distinct. A person who properly performs but one, attains the fruit of both. The status achieved by analytic methods is also attained by *yoga* practices. One who sees that analysis and practice are one [truly] sees" [5.4–5].

In other words, a spiritual practice (*yoga*) based on working in the world is better than scholarly study that is devoid of such spiritual practice [6.46]. Likewise, since all offerings and rites culminate in knowledge, a practice with knowledge is better than mere external rites [4.33].

Those striving on a disciplined spiritual path come to see the soul, whereas the undutiful, though striving, cannot see this, for they lack awareness [5.11]. One cannot merely study, for example, the problem of duality; one must rise above duality

---

[1] *The word niṣṭhā* is formed from *ni* (down or in) and *sthā* (status or standing). Thus *ni-ṣṭhā* indicates "a firm standing or position [on the spiritual plane]" and hence "devotion." The prefix *ni* is also found in *san-ni-āsa*, or *sannyāsa*, "renunciation."

by spiritual practice. Similarly, one may study God's nature, but devoted practice empowers one to see the higher spiritual nature and thus let go of lower attachments [2.59]. All spiritual paths taught in the *Gītā*, sincerely practiced, lead to a direct experience of the soul and God [13.25].

Thus true *karma-yoga* leads to spiritual knowledge and sincere *jñāna-yoga* leads one to act spiritually in the world. After all, it is our knowledge of life, and the goal of that knowledge, that inspire us to act [18.18].

Hence the philosophical tend to *knowledge-yoga* [3.3]. Pursuing knowledge as a spiritual path, and not merely for intellectual gratification, shows one's godly nature [16.1-3]. But what kind of knowledge do the knowledge-*yogīs* seek?

Let us examine Kṛṣṇa's description of knowledge: its structure and sources, its teachers and students, its experiential quality, its power to liberate, and its status as a sacred offering. We will consider these in turn.

Knowledge is like the sun: it destroys darkness and illumines all [5.16]. The sun rises gradually, spreading light evenly, even before it emerges above the horizon. Similarly, enlightenment may take time [6.45], yet the knowledge path gives us light and joy from the very start of our practice [9.2], even before we actually see God as Arjuna did.

Kṛṣṇa further states that He is giving all basic knowledge [7.2], and that one can personally realize this knowledge [9.2]. Let us now consider the structure of spiritual knowledge.

True Principles of Life (*Tattva*)

Kṛṣṇa claims to teach the best of all knowledge [14.1], knowing which there remains nothing more to be known [7.2]. Clearly Kṛṣṇa speaks here of the basic principles of knowledge, not all the details of earth's hundreds of sciences and disciplines.

In Sanskrit, the word *satyam* means *truth*, in the simple sense that a statement or concept is *true*, not false.[2] However the word *tattva*,[3] also often translated as *truth*, indicates a real, basic and demonstrable principle or category of existence.

Kṛṣṇa uses this term *tattva* throughout the *Gītā*. Clearly when Kṛṣṇa states that He is giving all knowledge, He means that He is giving all the main *tattvas*—or true, real principles of life. Thus when Arjuna asks Kṛṣṇa to explain knowledge [13.1], Kṛṣṇa responds categorically. Knowledge is to know three fundamental realities: 1) the material body (or material nature); 2) the soul, who knows the body; and, 3) God, who knows all bodies [13.2–3].

Then He concludes: "seeing the value of knowing truth—this is declared to be knowledge (*tattva*)" [13.12]. Conversely, "knowledge . . . that is meager and lacks a sense of truth (*tattva*) is declared to be in darkness" [18.22].

Thus the main *tattva*s (or realities) are nature, soul and God. And *Bhagavad-gītā*, which thoroughly explains nature, soul and God, is the highest knowledge [14.1]. One who studies this immortal dialogue engages in its *knowledge-offering* [18.70], as explained in the section on *yajña*.

It is thus not surprising that Kṛṣṇa often tells us that we must understand His teachings, "*tattvataḥ*"—i.e., according to fundamental, real principles (*tattva*s). Let us review Kṛṣṇa's use of this word.

---

[2] Kṛṣṇa uses the word in this way at 10.4, 16.2, 16.7, 16.8, 17.15 and 18.65.

[3] *Tattva* is formed from *tat*, "that," and *tva*, a suffix similar to the English suffix *ness* which denotes "a state or condition." *Tat* is a neuter demonstrative pronoun that, in this context, refers to a real object that can be demonstrated to exist. *Tat-tva* thus means "the state or condition of being a real, demonstrable object"—i.e., "a true ontological principle."

Matter and Spirit

Kṛṣṇa first uses the term *tattva* early in His teachings, saying that "truth-seers" (i.e., "*tattva*-seers") have seen that eternal things (like souls and God) never perish, while temporary things (like bodies and other material objects) never endure [2.16]. The entire *Gītā* builds upon this crucial distinction.

Similarly, when, by diligent spiritual practice, soul finally sees itself and knows the highest bliss, soul then never strays from *tattva*, true principles of reality [6.20–21].

Guṇa-karma

Tattva also relates to knowing the inner workings of the giant illusion machine called the universe. Thus a *tattva*-knower does not cling to mundane modal actions, knowing that in all such actions "modes are acting in modes" [3.28]. Knowing that soul is one *tattva* and that matter (with all its modes) is another, a *tattva*-knower does not cling to modal actions, for an action in which the body's modes interact with the world's modes is not truly soul's action (as has been elaborately explained above).

Similarly, even while performing such basic acts as seeing, hearing, touching, smelling, eating, etc., a *tattva*-knower should think, "I do nothing at all" [5.8]. Why? Because "the senses are moving in sense objects" [5.9] and the body's senses are not the soul. Body and soul are different *tattva*s.

Tattva also can refer to the true components of specific actions. Thus, as the *Gītā*'s final chapter opens, Arjuna wants to know by true principles (by *tattva*) what it means to renounce the world [18.1], since he famously misunderstood this topic at the start.

Kṛṣṇa-tattva

Kṛṣṇa uses the word *tattva* fifteen times in the *Gītā*, with more than half of these referring to the *Gītā*'s ultimate *topic*—Kṛṣṇa Himself. Thus:

One secures liberation from birth and death simply by knowing Kṛṣṇa's divine birth and deeds *in truth* (by *tattva*) [4.9]—i.e., knowing that they are not comparable to our own mundane birth and actions.

Tattva-seers have knowledge and help us to know and see that all souls exist in Kṛṣṇa, Soul of all [4.34–35].

Only one among thousands of successful spiritual practitioners knows Kṛṣṇa *in truth* (by *tattva*) [7.3].

They fall who do not recognize *in truth* (by *tattva*) that Kṛṣṇa is the Lord and Enjoyer of all offerings [9.24].

One who knows *in truth* (by *tattva*) Kṛṣṇa's vast power and *yoga* engages in unwavering *yoga* [10.7].

By pure devotion it is possible to know and see Kṛṣṇa *in truth* (by *tattva*) [11.54].

By devotion one recognizes *in truth* (by *tattva*) what Kṛṣṇa really is; thus knowing Him *in truth* (by *tattva*), one attains Him [18.55].

The pursuit of knowledge as a spiritual path (*jñāna-yoga*) ultimately aims at the highest knowable object: Kṛṣṇa. Thus, after many births, one who achieves knowledge knows that Kṛṣṇa is all and thus surrenders to Kṛṣṇa [7.19]. For *vedya* ("that which is to be known") is Kṛṣṇa [9.17, 11.38, 15.15] and *jñeyam* (also "that which is to be known") is Kṛṣṇa [13.13–18].

In Chapter 14, Kṛṣṇa declares that He will again give "the best of all knowledge" [14.1]: undeviating devotion to Kṛṣṇa lifts one above all material modes and brings one to pure spiritual existence [14.26], for Kṛṣṇa is the foundation of *brahman* (absolute spirit), and of unperishing immortality, everlasting virtue and highest bliss [14.27].

The attainment of profound spiritual knowledge, however, requires teamwork between *scripture*, *teacher* and *student*, all three of which must properly play their part. Let us now separately consider each member of this "*knowledge team.*"

Scripture (*Veda, Śāstra, Gītā*)

Kṛṣṇa emphatically teaches that even within the sacred Vedic tradition, not all scriptures are created equal. Dedicated to our spiritual emancipation, Kṛṣṇa ranks sacred texts not dogmatically, but by their transparently mundane or spiritual content. Kṛṣṇa speaks of scripture in three ways: 1) He speaks of Veda (or Vedas), usually pejoratively; 2) He speaks of *śāstra* (scripture), always positively; and, 3) He speaks of His own teaching, *Bhagavad-gītā*, as the *highest scripture*. One would expect no less from a text personally delivered by God. Let us review Kṛṣṇa's threefold reference to sacred texts.

Veda

The first ten times Kṛṣṇa mentions the Vedas,[4] He warns us away from them. Why? The Vedas, and many other scriptures, promote numerous rites that offer material rewards (e.g., celestial hedonism) to mundane minds eager for *good-karma fruits* [2.42–43].

We must keep in mind that *Bhagavad-gītā* and spiritual texts like *Śrīmad-bhāgavatam* describe both a mundane heaven within this temporal universe *and* a truly spiritual and eternal world beyond. This world's heaven offers but fleeting pleasure [9.21]. Indeed one cannot stay forever in any world in this universe [8.16]. Therefore, out of concern for us, Kṛṣṇa warns us away from all scriptures that promote this or that rite, vow or credence as a pathway to selfish pleasures.

---

[4] Vedas, in this context, indicate the four ancient ritual texts *Ṛg-veda, Yajur-veda, Sāma-veda* and *Atharva-veda*. Kṛṣṇa will make clear what the problem is.

In this way, Kṛṣṇa declares that the Vedas mainly focus on nature's three modes, urging Arjuna to transcend them [2.45]. And since spiritual devotion to Kṛṣṇa also brings material welfare [9.22], "all the Vedas have as much value as a well where, all about, wide waters stream" [2.46]. In other words, they have no value at all. One whose reason has crossed beyond illusion turns a deaf ear to Vedas, or to any scripture that sings the siren song of mundane life goals [2.52]. When such sacred *deals* no longer deviate the soul, then one achieves real spiritual *yoga* [2.53].

Kṛṣṇa continues his critique of the Vedas: a *yogī* who learns from Kṛṣṇa how to transcend this world, also transcends the Vedas [8.28]. Those who study the Vedas, perform the solemn rites and journey to this world's heaven, relish celestial treats; but they come crashing back down to earth when their *good-karma account* is spent [9.20–21]. As one would rationally expect, no one can see God through such Vedas [11.48, 11.53].

In Chapter Fifteen, however, Kṛṣṇa shows us the Vedas through another lens. The true Veda-knower knows that this world resembles an upside down tree [15.1]—i.e., it is a mere reflection of spiritual reality. In fact, all the Vedas are meant to know Kṛṣṇa and Kṛṣṇa knows the Vedas [15.15]. Here we find an apparent contradiction: on the one hand, Kṛṣṇa tells Arjuna that the Vedas mainly range through nature's three modes [2.45], and on the other, Kṛṣṇa proclaims that all the Vedas aim at Him, Who is beyond the modes [7.13]. How can this be?

We can trace an answer in the *Gītā* itself. Consider these statements:

1. One who knows spirit and matter—*including the modes*—does not take birth again [13.24].
2. One who sees that modes instigate all mundane actions, *and who sees what is beyond the modes*, achieves My own nature [14.19].

3. Transcending these three modes, one is freed from the miseries of birth, death and old age and enjoys the immortal [14.20].

Thus, in the greater scheme of things, the Vedas lead us through nature's modes, but the ultimate goal is to transcend those modes and know Kṛṣṇa, who is beyond them [7.13].

Conclusion: though the Vedas speak much more of this world than of God, they still ultimately point to Kṛṣṇa by occasional references to Viṣṇu [Kṛṣṇa] as a transcendent being[5] who embodies the liberating act of sacrifice,[6] or by showing us the ultimate futility of mundane rewards.

Also, the word *veda* literally means *knowledge*; so Kṛṣṇa is literally saying at 15.15 that "all forms of *knowledge* are meant to know Me."

In any case, in His last explicit mention of the Vedas, Kṛṣṇa says: "In the world and in the Vedas I am celebrated as the Supreme Person" [15.18].

Śāstra

Having surveyed Kṛṣṇa's explicit discussion of the Vedas, let us look at Kṛṣṇa's five uses of the term *śāstra*, a more generic term meaning *scripture*, in the sense of a divine authoritative text.

Having explained that He is the Supreme Person beyond all other souls, bound or liberated, Kṛṣṇa states that He has spoken "most confidential *śāstra*" [15.20].

One who rejects *śāstra*'s commands lives by selfish acts and cannot achieve perfection, happiness or the highest path [16.23].

---

[5] *Ṛg-veda* 1.22.17, 1.22,18, 1.154.2, 1.156.4, etc.

[6] *Taittarīya Saṁhitā* 5.5.1.4., etc.

Therefore *śāstra* is our evidence in determining what is and is not to be done. Knowing what *śāstra* enjoins, we should do our duty [16.24].

Hearing this, Arjuna asks about those who reject *śāstra*'s commands but still make offerings with faith. Is their status goodness, passion or ignorance [17.1]? Interestingly, Arjuna assumes that one who gives up *śāstra*'s commands cannot be a liberated soul, and so he asks in which way such a person is bound to nature's modes. Kṛṣṇa replies that it depends on the individual.

He also states that only those who ignore *śāstra*'s rules perform injurious penance [17.5]; *śāstra* never enjoins us to harm ourselves.

Unlike His mixed treatment of the Vedas, Kṛṣṇa always refers to *śāstra* as positive and authoritative. And He describes His own teaching as the highest, or most confidential, *śāstra*.

Bhagavad-gītā

Since Kṛṣṇa is the source of everything [10.8], and since both matter and spirit, the twin components of the cosmos, are His energy [7.4–5], Kṛṣṇa is, in *that* sense, everything [7.19, 11.40]. Thus we cannot truly or finally understand anything unless we also understand Kṛṣṇa. And if we wish to understand Kṛṣṇa, a few common sense epistemic rules apply:

1. Since Kṛṣṇa is the source of gods and great sages, they do not know His origin [10.2]. Why then look when even gods and enlightened sages cannot find it?
2. The highest cosmic beings do not know Kṛṣṇa's personal form by their own efforts [10.14]. Again, we should be realistic about our chances.
3. Only Kṛṣṇa truly knows Himself [10.15].

4. Kṛṣṇa is willing to fully explain Himself to us if we will only listen [7.1]; thus Kṛṣṇa spoke *Bhagavad-gītā*.
5. To understand the *Gītā*, we must hear it through the authorized chain of teachers called *paramparā* [4.1–3].

Kṛṣṇa assures us that He will give us all basic knowledge with deep realization [7.2]. This realized knowledge will lead us to spiritual liberation [9.1]. Indeed, since we cannot see Kṛṣṇa with our material eyes, Kṛṣṇa can give us divine vision, as He did for Arjuna, so that we can actually see Him [11.8].

Kṛṣṇa implores us to listen to His supreme word, which He speaks for our good [10.1]. He offers the best of all knowledge—wisdom that has led all previous sages to perfection [14.1]. But Kṛṣṇa can only offer; thus He tells Arjuna at the end: "I have explained to you most confidential knowledge. Considering it carefully, do as you wish" [18.63].

That would appear to be the last word. But so earnest is Kṛṣṇa in His wish to help us that having just told Arjuna to do as he wishes, He then says: "I love you dearly, so again I will speak for your good. Listen once more to My supreme word" [18.64].

Spiritual Teachers

God's Representatives

I mentioned above that we are to receive this knowledge through *paramparā*, the continuous chain of authorized teachers [4.1–3]. The knowledge descends from Kṛṣṇa in this unbroken living chain.

We find three examples of *paramparā* in the *Gītā*:

1. Of old, Kṛṣṇa taught Vivasvān, who taught his son Manu, who taught his son Ikṣvāku [4.1–2].

2. Kṛṣṇa renews the lost succession by speaking to Arjuna [4.3].
3. Sañjaya, who begins and ends the *Gītā*, hears Kṛṣṇa speak by the mercy of *his* teacher Vyāsa [18.75].

Kṛṣṇa explains why He chose Arjuna to personally hear His regenerative narration of the *Gītā*: Arjuna is Kṛṣṇa's devotee and friend [4.3]. When one's mind clings to Kṛṣṇa, and one takes shelter of Him, Kṛṣṇa gives all knowledge, explaining how one can know Him fully beyond doubt [7.1–2].

Further, to those who steadily love Him, Kṛṣṇa personally gives *buddhi-yoga*, spiritual intelligence by which they come to Him [10.10]. Out of compassion for them, He destroys their ignorance with the shining lamp of knowledge [10.11]. Thus Kṛṣṇa says: "My devotee fully understands this knowledge" [13.19].

Clearly, to fully understand *Bhagavad-gītā* one must know Kṛṣṇa; and one who loves Kṛṣṇa can know Him. Is Kṛṣṇa partial to devotees and unfair to others? He addresses this question, saying that He is equal to all beings, neither hating nor favoring anyone. Yet He abides in those who abide in Him [9.29]. He fairly reciprocates with everyone [4.11], as we explained in the section on God.

Many people today claim to know the *Gītā*, and thus to be qualified *gurus*, spiritual teachers. Clearly, Kṛṣṇa teaches that one who follows Arjuna, one who is Kṛṣṇa's devotee and friend, can know *Bhagavad-gītā*. Yet many claim to be, among other things, Kṛṣṇa's devotee, and thus to have deep spiritual knowledge. So let us consider how Kṛṣṇa describes the behavior and mentality of those who truly understand, serve and teach His message—i.e., those that are true teachers of the *Gītā*.

Seers of Categorical Truth

Twice in the *Gītā* Kṛṣṇa describes enlightened persons as *tattva-darśī*, "seers of [categorical] truth." Thus a *truth-seer* sees the difference between eternal things (souls) and temporary things (bodies) [2.16]. *Tattva-darśīs*, truth-seers, are qualified to teach us knowledge, for they have *realized* knowledge [4.34].

As explained earlier, there are three basic *tattvas* or fundamental truths: nature, souls and God. Thus a *tattva*-seer does not confuse these truths—i.e., a *tattva*-seer does not:

1. Confuse matter and spirit, thinking the eternal soul to be the temporary body.
2. Confuse spirit and God, thinking the soul to be God.
3. Confuse God and matter, thinking that Kṛṣṇa comes to this world in a material body or that any material object, even the material universe, is God in a simple unqualified sense.

Thus a knowing person must see, and not confuse, *tattvas*, basic truths. Fortunately, Kṛṣṇa also gives us behavioral symptoms by which we can recognize the truly wise teacher, and thus pursue a type of spiritual science.

Behavioral Symptoms of the Truly Wise

Twice Arjuna asks Kṛṣṇa about the qualities and behavior of a person who has truly realized spiritual knowledge. Here we have the makings of a spiritual science with observable principles.

In the first case Arjuna asks about the behavior of one fixed in wisdom. Kṛṣṇa replies that a wise person gives up all selfish desires, finds satisfaction in self alone [2.55], lives free of yearning, passion, fear and anger [2.56], and neither welcomes good fortune nor despises bad fortune [2.57]. One with knowledge withdraws the senses from sense objects like a turtle retracts its limbs [2.58]. True detachment requires genuine experience of something higher; otherwise, one will return to lower pleasures [2.59]. Thus steady detachment from mundane gratification is a valid sign of spiritual attachment, as much as giving up one's childhood toys is a sign that one is growing and maturing.

In the second case Kṛṣṇa states that by transcending the three material modes one is freed from birth, death and old-age miseries, and enjoys immortality [14.20]. Arjuna then asks about the symptoms of such a person [14.21]. Kṛṣṇa again replies that the liberated soul is revealed by full detachment from worldly modes, and from dualities such as joy and sorrow, censure and praise, honor and dishonor, the pleasing and the displeasing [14.23–25]. Kṛṣṇa adds that one who serves the Lord with undeviating *bhakti-yoga* fully transcends the modes and attains the Absolute [14.26].

Further, Kṛṣṇa twice gives an extensive list of qualities, characteristics, habits and traits entailed by true knowledge. First He speaks of pridelessness, non-duplicity, not harming, forgiveness, rectitude, serving spiritual guides, cleanliness, steadiness, self-control and many other such traits, concluding that *this is knowledge*; *what is otherwise, is ignorance* [13.8–12].

Similarly, the highest status of knowledge, leading to spiritual existence, includes characteristics like pure reason, determined self-control, giving up attachment and aversion, light eating, dedication to meditation-*yoga* and many others [18.50–53]. Ultimately, as mentioned above, a person with true knowledge realizes that the Lord is everything, and thus surrenders to Him [7.19].

Here it is important to note that the above descriptions nowhere indicate that a soul with knowledge withdraws from the world. On the contrary, those in knowledge still perform duties according to their bodily nature [3.33]. To know God is not to deny the body, but rather to govern and engage it in a reasonable, spiritual way. As discussed earlier, true renunciation is to renounce action's fruits [18.2]. And what better example than Arjuna himself, who, with knowledge restored, declares to Kṛṣṇa at the end: "I stand firm, free of doubt. I shall *act* upon Your word" [18.73].

Lastly, Kṛṣṇa describes the vision and behavior of a *paṇḍita*,[7] a truly learned person:

A *paṇḍita* laments neither for souls still in bodies nor for souls that leave their bodies [2.11].

A *paṇḍita* undertakes all actions without selfish motive, for knowledge has burnt up all *karma* [4.19].

A *paṇḍita* sees that philosophy and practice are one [5.4].

A *paṇḍita* sees the equality of all souls, despite the difference of body in terms of species, gender or social class [5.18].

Sincere Students

If we are so fortunate as to find a true teacher of *Bhagavad-gītā*, how do we approach that person? The *Gītā* itself clearly shows us, first by Arjuna's example and then in Kṛṣṇa's teachings on the duties of a spiritual student.

After failing to enlighten himself in Chapter One, Arjuna realizes that he needs a perfect teacher, and says to Kṛṣṇa: ". . . Baffled about duty, I inquire as to that which is the certain good? Tell me, I am your disciple; teach me, for I am surrendered to you" [2.7].

Arjuna declares himself a submissive disciple, but freely expresses his doubts, posing challenging questions [3.1–2, 5.1] before accepting all that Kṛṣṇa has told [10.14] and agreeing to execute His command [18.73].

Here Arjuna's relationship with Kṛṣṇa matches Kṛṣṇa's own description of a proper teacher-student relationship: one should approach a wise teacher (*tattva*-seer) with submission, thorough questions and devoted service. This attitude naturally induces the wise to teach us all they know [4.34].

---

[7] The Sanskrit word *paṇḍita* has come into English as *pundit*.

Ultimately, one who trusts Kṛṣṇa's message attains knowledge, and that knowledge brings supreme peace [4.39]. Depending on that knowledge, one is united with Kṛṣṇa [14.2]. One should strive to be like Arjuna, Kṛṣṇa's most famous student.

Seeing the Truth (*Dṛṣṭi*)

Because Arjuna does not envy God, Kṛṣṇa teaches him liberating knowledge that one can grasp by direct perception [9.2]. Throughout the *Gītā*, Kṛṣṇa makes clear that to deeply know Truth is to *see* Truth. Kṛṣṇa's message is strikingly visual. Faith leads to knowledge [4.39], but knowledge itself must be seen, not merely believed. Only upon *seeing* higher truth can one give up mundane sense objects [2.59]. Let us now summarize the role of *spiritual seeing* in the *Gītā*.

As discussed earlier, Kṛṣṇa twice speaks of *truth-* or *tattva-seers* that have *seen* the conclusion of matter and spirit: material forms never endure, spirit never perishes [2.16]. Similarly, *tattva-seers* see that all souls exist within Kṛṣṇa [4.34–35]. And knowledge entails *seeing* the need to know *tattva*: fundamental, categorical truth [13.12].

Kṛṣṇa speaks often of *seeing* the basic realities of soul, nature and God, and not confusing them. Thus some *see* that soul is wonderful [2.29]; and one finds satisfaction upon *seeing* true self, by self, within oneself [6.20].

One must also see what is not truth. Thus, by the *knowledge-eye*, one attains the supreme upon *realizing* the difference between body and soul and *seeing* how to free oneself from matter [13.35]. Similarly, knowledge entails steadily *seeing* the miserable problem of birth, death, old age and disease [13.9], since this motivates one to seek liberation. And the seeing sage *sees* the world's pleasures as darkness, just as the ordinary world *sees* the saintly life as inscrutable [2.69].

One who *sees* oneself as the only doer does not actually *see* [18.16]; but one who *sees* that nature is conducting actions, and that self is a non-doer, *truly sees* [13.30]. Similarly, one who steadily *sees* no doer beyond nature's modes, and also *sees* what is beyond those modes, attains My existence [14.19].

The bewildered do not *see* the soul leaving, inhabiting or enjoying the physical body, but those with a *knowledge-eye* do *see* [15.10]. Striving *yogīs see* self in Self; but even striving, the undutiful do not *see*, for they lack awareness [15.11].

Various spiritual paths taught in the *Gītā*—meditation-*yoga*, knowledge-*yoga*, action-*yoga*, etc.—all enable one to *see* true self within oneself, by oneself [13.25]. Similarly, one who *sees* that philosophy (*jñāna-yoga*) and practice (*karma-yoga*) are one, truly *sees* [5.5].

We discussed earlier that Kṛṣṇa defines *yoga* as *equal vision*, and He emphasizes that we must *see* the equality of all beings, beyond bodily differences. Thus one who learns from the wise *sees* all beings, without exception, within Kṛṣṇa, the Supreme Soul [4.35]. A wise person, a *paṇḍita*, *sees* all creatures equally, despite their social class or species [5.18]. A soul engaged on the spiritual path *sees* the soul in all beings, and all beings in the Soul, and thus *sees* equally everywhere [6.29]. That is, one *sees* Kṛṣṇa everywhere, and everything in Kṛṣṇa [6.30]. Kṛṣṇa makes this point elsewhere as well [9.5, 13.28–29].

Kṛṣṇa indirectly speaks of knowledge as *seeing* when He states that soul has knowledge by nature (*jñānin*) but that ignorance *covers* or *conceals* it. Thus five times in the *Gītā* Kṛṣṇa states that knowledge is *covered* or *concealed* (*āvṛtam*)[8]: by lust and anger [3.38]; by our eternal enemy lust [3.39 and 3.40]; by "*unknowledge*" (*ajñāna*) or ignorance [5.15]; and, by darkness [14.9].

Light discovers what darkness covers. Thus, by dispelling the world's darkness, the sun enables us to see. Kṛṣṇa

---

[8]Using a form of the same word, Kṛṣṇa says that He is *concealed* (*samāvṛta*) by His own mystic power, not by ignorance [7.25].

twice compares knowledge (awareness) to the sun: when our knowledge destroys ignorance, then that knowledge, like the sun, illumines all around it [5.16]; just as one sun illumines this entire world, so the knowing soul, owner of the field (body), illumines the entire field [13.34].

However, nature's lower modes of passion and ignorance cover the soul's innate knowledge. But the highest mode, virtue or goodness, permits the light of knowledge to shine, enabling us to see. Thus four verses explicitly link virtue or goodness to higher knowledge: goodness, being unsullied, enlightens [14.6]; when all the body's gates (senses) are illumined, when there is knowledge, then one should know that goodness prospers [14.11]; when the converse occurs—when there is no light—then the darkness mode prospers [14.13]; indeed the light of knowledge symptomizes virtue [14.22].

Essentially, virtue's knowledge is to *see* that all beings, with their distinct natures, stand as one in the vast spiritual field of *brahman* [13.31]. Similarly, such virtuous knowledge *sees* a single unperishing spiritual nature, undivided in all the divided living beings [18.20]. Kṛṣṇa describes only knowledge in goodness as *seeing*.

A person immersed in passion and ignorance may learn many things, but will not *see* the spiritual truth within all beings. Thus passionate, ignorant thinkers deny the soul and God because they can *see* neither.

Kṛṣṇa warns that nature's modes cover our vision of God [7.13]. To actually *see* truth that will set us free, we must seek knowledge (*jñāna*) within a spiritual practice (*yoga*)—i.e., *jñāna-yoga*. By this we systematically peel off cognitive coverings that conceal pure awareness. In gross consciousness, we cannot understand Spirit, which is most subtle, existing within and without all beings [13.16].

Bhagavad-gītā most powerfully reveals knowledge as direct *seeing* in Chapter Eleven, when Kṛṣṇa unveils His cosmic form to the astounded Arjuna. In twenty-four of that chapter's fifty-five verses, we find forty usages of the verb "*to see*" (*paśya*) in various forms. Kṛṣṇa, Arjuna and Sañjaya, who begins and ends the *Gītā*, all use *seeing* words extensively. Again and again, Kṛṣṇa tells Arjuna, "*See!*" [11.5–7], and Arjuna repeatedly declares, "*I see!*" [11.15–19]. This is no ordinary vision, for Arjuna sees the entire cosmos present in one place—i.e., within God's body [11.7.13]. (I explained more about Arjuna's vision in the section on God.)

Knowledge that Liberates

Just as Janaka and other great kings achieved full perfection by *karma-yoga* [3.23], so *Bhagavad-gītā* teaches that knowledge will set us free from all evil—from sins and the misfortune they cause us. Nothing purifies like knowledge [4.38]. Knowledge is the supreme purifier [9.2]. By the knowledge-boat alone even the most sinful person will cross over all evil [4.36]. Knowledge shakes off all sins [5.17]. Kṛṣṇa teaches the most confidential knowledge, knowing which one is free from sin [9.1]. Knowing Kṛṣṇa as the unborn, beginningless great Lord of the worlds, one is free from all sins [10.3].

Thus freeing us from sin, knowledge frees us from repeated birth and death. One who truly knows soul and nature never takes birth again [13.24]. Even unknowing persons who faithfully hear this knowledge actually cross over death [13.26].

Material acts bind us and spiritual acts free us. Thus one who knows *karma* and non-*karma* is freed from evil [4.16]. The most liberating action is *yajña*, sacrifice, and one who knows this is liberated [4.32]. A *yogī* who knows the right way to leave this world attains the highest place [8.28].

Knowledge is a fire that burns up our *karma* [4.19]. Just as blazing fire turns wood to ashes, so knowledge-fire turns all *karma* to ashes [4.37]. Thus, on attaining knowledge, one quickly achieves highest peace [4.39]. Those who know, with the *knowledge-eye*, the difference between body and soul, and the path to freedom from matter, go to the Supreme [13.35]. Similarly, those with the *knowledge-eye* see how the soul accepts, enjoys and leaves a body [15.10].

Kṛṣṇa teaches highest knowledge, knowing which all the sages reached highest perfection [14.1]. And just as neither this world nor the next is for one who makes no offering [4.31], so neither this world nor one higher is for a doubting soul without knowledge [4.40]. But one who is devoted to the Lord understands body and soul, and thus attains the Lord's nature [13.19].

Knowledge cuts away doubt [4.41]. Doubt arises from not knowing, but the *knowledge-sword* severs the soul's doubt [4.42]. Knowledge of Kṛṣṇa is especially potent; realizing that Kṛṣṇa is beyond *karma*, one is also freed from *karma* [4.14]. Attaining knowledge, one never again falls into illusion, for one will see that all beings are in Kṛṣṇa, the Soul [4.35]. And after many births, one who actually attains knowledge surrenders to Kṛṣṇa, knowing that Vasudeva's son[9] is everything [7.19].

The Knowledge-Offering (*Jñāna-yajña*)

Centered on intellectual engagement, knowledge-*yoga* (*jñāna-yoga*), just like action-*yoga* (*karma-yoga*), contains all of *yoga*'s universal features, including the rule of offering one's practice to God. Thus Kṛṣṇa speaks four times of *jñāna-yajña*, the "knowledge offering."[10] What then is a *knowledge offering*?

Consider the archetypal offering: God-given rain [9.19] makes God-given seeds grow [7.10, 10.39], providing food that we

[9] "Vasudeva's son" is a reference to Kṛṣṇa, who appeared as the son of the Yadu prince Vasudeva.

[10] 4.28, 4.33, 9.15, 18.70.

consume with God-given digestion [15.15], inspiring a grateful offering to the giver [3.11–12, 3.14–15].

Similarly, the thinker thinks with God-given intelligence [7.10, 10.32], given by Kṛṣṇa within our heart [5.15]. Indeed, present within our heart, Kṛṣṇa *is* our knowledge, the knowable, and all that is attained by knowledge [13.18]. Kṛṣṇa is also *that which is to be known* [9.17, 11.38], *the supreme knowable* [11.18], and the *only object of knowledge* in "knowledge books" (Vedas) [15.15].

As with the body's food, the mind's food too is God-given, and obviously calls for a grateful offering. Thus by *jñāna-yajña* (the knowledge-offering), we thank Kṛṣṇa for our intelligence and knowledge, and we use those God-given faculties to know and understand their source: Kṛṣṇa Himself. Here too, we keep the cosmic cycle turning, receiving and gratefully offering back [3.16]. In fact, knowledge ignites the fire of *self-control yoga*, into which *yogīs* offer all sense and breath actions [4.27].

Kṛṣṇa first defines *jñāna-yajña* as *sacred study*, and includes it in a menu of sacrifices that *yogīs* may offer within their various practices [4.28]. The best example of a knowledge-offering is *Bhagavad-Gītā* itself. Kṛṣṇa states at the *Gītā*'s end that one who studies His dialogue with Arjuna truly makes a knowledge-offering to Kṛṣṇa [18.70]. Thus simply learning *Bhagavad-gītā* puts one firmly on the path to full knowledge.

Elsewhere Kṛṣṇa calls His teaching *yoga* [4.1–3]. Here again we find that *yoga* is a form of *yajña* (offering)—in this case, disciplined spiritual study done as an offering back to the source of all knowledge and the energy to learn it.

Kṛṣṇa knows and respects our different natures and so offers various physical, meditational and intellectual *yogas*; *but all are meant to be devoted offerings (yajña) and thus spiritual paths.* All practitioners who realize this common purpose achieve the Absolute [4.30]. Thus knowledge is key. An offering imbued with knowledge surpasses the mere offering of material goods [4.33].

Further, though many seek God to relieve their suffering or curiosity, or to gain prosperity, the best seeker is one who *knows* Kṛṣṇa's glory, and thus seeks Him with real understanding. Indeed, knowledge of God leads to singular devotion and constant engagement in His service [7.16–17].

PART X
Dhyāna-yoga (Meditation-*Yoga*)

Meditation as a Spiritual Practice

Apart from action-*yoga* and knowledge-*yoga* (*karma-yoga* and *jñāna-yoga*), *Bhagavad-gītā* teaches meditation-*yoga* (*dhyāna-yoga*). Just as action in the world must be spiritually transformed into action-*yoga*, or the pursuit of knowledge elevated to knowledge-*yoga*, so meditation should be spiritually transformed into meditation-*yoga*. Merely concentrating on this or that object may lead not to liberation, but to abject bondage. Thus Kṛṣṇa wryly refers to those who *meditate* on sense objects, become attached to them, and ultimately fall into deepest illusion [2.62–63]. Similarly, learning how and why to give up the fruit of one's work is better than merely meditating without such renunciation [12.12]. The *Gītā* thus teaches meditation-*yoga*, *dhyāna-yoga*.

Kṛṣṇa twice mentions this process by name, stating that *dhyāna-yoga*, like the other *yoga* paths, can enable one to see the true self [13.25], and thus can help one to reach pure spiritual existence [18.52].

Apart from these verses, Kṛṣṇa refers to meditation throughout the *Gītā*. The Sixth Chapter is often titled *Dhyāna-yoga* (Meditation-*yoga*), even though Kṛṣṇa does not use that specific term in the chapter. He does, however, say much about meditation as a spiritual practice.

Kṛṣṇa states where one should meditate: alone and in seclusion [6.10], in a pure place [6.11]. He then tells the *yogī* how to fashion a meditation seat: a firm seat, not too high or low, covered with deerskin and *kuśa* grass [6.11]. The *yogī* is then instructed to sit down, focus the mind on one point, restrain senses and activities, and practice *yoga* to purify self [6.12].

Kṛṣṇa next describes correct body alignment: one holds head, neck and body straight, steady and unmoving, staring at the tip of one's nose, and not glancing in other directions [6.13]. Serene, fearless, with a vow of celibacy, one should continue to engage the mind. Significantly, one is told to fix the mind on Kṛṣṇa, dedicating oneself to Him [6.14].

Clearly many people will find it impractical to live and practice *yoga* alone, in seclusion and with strict celibacy. Fortunately, Kṛṣṇa explains that one can practice *bhakti-yoga* (the highest *yoga*) [6.47] in the company of others, as opposed to seclusion [9.14, 10.9] and celibacy [3.20][1], which the *Gītā* requires for more technical, but in no way superior, forms of *yoga* [6.14, 8.11]. Kṛṣṇa also mentions celibacy as a type of bodily austerity, but not as a compulsory practice [17.14].

Kṛṣṇa completes His summary of classic *yoga* practice by explaining the need to moderate eating, recreation and sleeping [6.16], the symptoms of *yoga* serenity [6.19], the blissful state of enlightenment [6.20–23], steps of advanced meditation [6.24–26], higher achievements and contact with the Absolute [6.27–28], and seeing the Soul (Kṛṣṇa) in all beings and all beings in Kṛṣṇa, thus connecting irrevocably to the Lord [6.29–30] and developing universal empathy [6.32].

But Arjuna has a doubt: what if he gives up his worldly life, takes to *yoga* practice, but then fails. Wouldn't he then have spoiled both his material and his spiritual life, ending up with

[1] King Janaka, whom Kṛṣṇa cites here as exemplary, was a celebrated householder devotee, and father-in-law, of Lord Rāma, Who married Janaka's daughter Sītā.

nothing [6.33–35, 6.37–39]? Kṛṣṇa reassures Arjuna, explaining the glorious rewards that come to a sincere *yogī*, even one who sometimes falls short [6.35–36, 6.40–45].

Kṛṣṇa thus urges Arjuna to be a *yogī*, since this *yoga* path surpasses the paths of *karma*, *jñāna* and *tapas* (or asceticism) [6.46]. And lest we think that Kṛṣṇa is urging Arjuna to give up his warrior life, Kṛṣṇa reveals that Arjuna need neither go to a secluded place nor (as a married man) adopt celibacy in order to practice the highest *yoga*. In fact, of all *yogīs*, the most advanced is one whose inner self goes to Kṛṣṇa and who faithfully worships the Lord [6.47]. This certainly describes Arjuna, who Lord Kṛṣṇa spoke of as "My devotee and friend" [4.3].

As with the previous discussion on *karma-yoga* and *jñāna-yoga*, here too meditation-*yoga* culminates in devotion to Kṛṣṇa. Kṛṣṇa is the goal [6.15]. The *dhyāna-yogī* fixes the mind on Kṛṣṇa [6.15, 6.47], is dedicated to Him [6.14] and goes to Him [6.15].

Elsewhere Kṛṣṇa reiterates meditation's goal: the Lord personally uplifts from the *ocean of death-wandering* (the material world) the devoted that *meditate* upon Him exclusively, with full dedication [12.6–7].

Chapter Eight also revisits technical *dhyāna-yoga*, even citing auspicious and inauspicious times for *yogīs* to depart this world [8.23–27]. Here too, the meditating *yogī* should fix the mind on Kṛṣṇa [8.5,7], always thinking of Him as the Supreme Divine Person [8.8, 8.10], and as "the ancient seer and constant ruler, smaller than the smallest, creator of all, of inconceivable form, lustrous like the sun, beyond darkness" [8.9].

We should note that for an ordinary *dhyāna-yogī*, the technical time of departing determines whether one comes back to this world or goes beyond it. However, one who meditates on Kṛṣṇa while leaving this world will go to Kṛṣṇa [8.5], with no mention of technical time frames. Here love, not technique, conquers all.

Meditation as Spiritual Offering

As we would expect, there are also *yajña* options for meditating *yogīs*. Some, deep in meditation, offer the five senses into the symbolic fire of self-control, while others offer sense objects into the fire of the senses [4.26]. Some offer all sense and breath actions into self-control fire, made to blaze by knowledge [4.27]. For those dedicated to the breathing exercises of *prāṇāyāma*, one can offer in-breath to out-breath or out-breath to in-breath [4.29]. Thus even a *yogī* who lives on *air* gives thanks and offering for that air. Kṛṣṇa stresses that one who makes no offering can be neither a renunciate nor a *yogī* [6.1].

Even a detached wise *yogī* must offer. One can never renounce one's debt to the source of all, nor one's duty to help others, any more than one can renounce self-control. For these acts purify even the wise [18.5].

In reviewing Kṛṣṇa's teaching of various *yogas*, one may feel the need for more specific information on exactly how one practices these paths. In fact, it is *bhakti-yoga*, the highest of all *yogas* [6.47, 12.2], that clearly illumines what it means to *offer* action, knowledge or meditation to the Source and Supreme, and thus to transform action, knowledge and meditation into a true spiritual path.

In the final section, we will consider, in depth, the culmination of all spiritual paths: the path of pure love, *bhakti-yoga*. This is the heart of *Bhagavad-gītā*.

PART XI
Bhakti-yoga (The *Yoga* of Devotion)

Hierarchy of *Yogas* and *Yogīs*

Kṛṣṇa accepts several paths to freedom [5.4–5, 13.25, etc.], but He also ranks them:[1] inclusive and cosmopolitan, the *Gītā* recognizes that some points on the path are farther along than others. Thus an offering in knowledge surpasses mere ritual [4.33]; a *yogī* devoted to spiritual practice surpasses mere ascetics, scholars and ritualists [6.46]; and of all *yogīs*, one devoted heart and soul to Kṛṣṇa (the *bhakti-yogī*) is best [6.47].

Karma-yoga requires offering the fruits of our actions, and throughout the *Gītā* Kṛṣṇa requests us to offer all our actions to Him.[2] Similarly, *jñāna-yoga* culminates in Kṛṣṇa, as clearly shown in the section on knowledge-*yoga*. As for *dhyāna-yoga*, the path of mystic meditation, the *Gītā* teaches throughout that we must fix our mind on Kṛṣṇa.[3] Ultimately action-*yoga*, knowledge-*yoga* and the *yoga* of meditation all find their perfection in pure love of God and all His creatures: *bhakti*.

Kṛṣṇa defined *yoga* as *samatvam*, equality, and that equality rests on Kṛṣṇa's equal presence everywhere, as shown earlier. Kṛṣṇa also defines *yoga* as *sannyāsa*, giving up or unto, and ultimately one should give all unto Kṛṣṇa with devotion

---

[1] 4.33 6.46, 12.1–3, 12.8–12, etc.

[2] 3.30, 9.27, 12.6, 12.10, 18.56, 18.57.

[3] Here are some examples: 6.14–15, 6.31, 7.1, 7.7, 8.7, 10.9, 12.2, 12.8, 12.14, 13.11 and 19.57.

(*bhakti*), again, as shown earlier. And the disciplined spiritual path that directly focuses on *bhakti* is, of course, *bhakti-yoga*.

The word *bhakti* comes from the verbal root *bhaj*: *to serve, honor, revere, love, adore*. Thus to serve, honor, revere, love and adore God is *bhakti*. One who performs *bhakti* is a *bhakta*, a devoted one.

Often in the *Gītā*, Kṛṣṇa refers to "*My devotees*."[4] Kṛṣṇa does not so identify with mystic *yogīs* or sages who do not love Him. Rather the *Gītā* states about the devoted that they truly grasp the *Gītā* [4.3, 13.19], they attain Kṛṣṇa [7.23, 9.34, 11.55, 18.65, etc.], they are never lost [9.31], they are dear to Kṛṣṇa [12.14, 12.16], indeed exceedingly dear [12.20], and they render the highest devotion by teaching *Bhagavad-gītā* to other devoted souls [18.68].

Bhagavad-gītā reserves the term *mahātmā*, "great soul," for Kṛṣṇa [11.13,20,37,50] *and* Kṛṣṇa's devotees [7.19, 8.15, 9.13], especially Arjuna [18.74]. Vedas, austerity, charity and sacrifice do not empower one to see Kṛṣṇa; only pure devotion reveals the Lord [11.54]. In fact, Kṛṣṇa finally exhorts Arjuna to teach the *Gītā* only to the devoted [18.67].

Why does Kṛṣṇa prioritize devotion so dramatically? Why does He claim that *bhakti-yoga* is the highest *yoga* path? In making these claims, does He remain true to His promise that He is equal to everyone, neither favoring nor hating anyone [9.29], and fairly reciprocating with all [4.11]?

To answer this, and thus penetrate to the heart of *Bhagavad-gītā*, we must look closely at the *Gītā*'s highest spiritual path, *bhakti-yoga*: the disciplined cultivation of pure spiritual love.

Knowledge of Kṛṣṇa

Kṛṣṇa discusses many topics in the *Gītā*, but clearly the ultimate topic is Kṛṣṇa Himself. Indeed, in ten of the *Gītā*'s

---

[4] 4.3, 7.23, 9.31, 9.34, 11.55, 12.14, 12.16, 12.20, 13.19, 18.65, 18.68.

eighteen chapters, the final, conclusive verse[5] urges readers to understand or devote themselves to Kṛṣṇa, the Supreme God, Source of all, who literally makes the world go round [9.10].

Kṛṣṇa Himself is the object of knowledge: *that which is to be known;*[6] the *supreme object of knowledge* [11.18], the true *knowable of all books of knowledge* [15.15], and that which is to be attained by knowledge [13.18].

Thus one may take to the path of devotion, *bhakti-yoga*, as a natural response to knowledge. For example, "after many births, one in knowledge surrenders to Kṛṣṇa, realizing that He is everything" [7.19]. Similarly, realizing that Kṛṣṇa is the source of all, and that all emanates from Him, the rational adore Kṛṣṇa with much feeling [10.8]. And one who clearly knows Kṛṣṇa as the Supreme Person, knows all, and adores Him with all one's being [15.19].

Just as knowledge inspires *bhakti*, devotion, so *bhakti* may also invoke knowledge. Thus, because Arjuna is His devoted (*bhakta*) friend, Kṛṣṇa teaches him the mysteries of *Bhagavad-gītā* [4.3]. Not only to Arjuna, but also to all who are ever devoted with love, Kṛṣṇa gives the intelligence (*buddhi-yoga*) by which they attain Him [10.10]; present within them, Kṛṣṇa destroys their ignorance with the shining knowledge lamp [10.11].

Only pure devotion empowers one to know Kṛṣṇa, and thus to see and approach Him in truth [11.54]. And it is Kṛṣṇa's devotee who understands the truth of body and soul, characterized as *field* and *field-knower* [13.19].

Toward the *Gītā*'s end [11.55], Kṛṣṇa repeats the word *tattvataḥ* (by true principles) to emphasize that devotion (*bhakti*) enables one to know Him categorically. Those who lack spiritual discernment—not knowing Kṛṣṇa's higher nature (*param bhāvam ajānantaḥ*) as the great Lord of all beings—believe that

[5] 5.29, 6.47, 7.30, 9.34, 10.42, 11.55, 12.20, 14.27, 15.20, 18.78.

[6] 9.17, 11.38, 13.1, 13.13, 13.17, 13.18.

Kṛṣṇa is originally an impersonal existence that has taken on a personal feature [7.24]; thus they minimize Kṛṣṇa when He appears in His human-like form [9.11]. In other words, the devoted do not confuse spirit and matter, and thus know Kṛṣṇa rightly and categorically—*tattvataḥ*. Such knowledge liberates the soul from matter.

What does it mean here to know *categorically*? As explained earlier, Kṛṣṇa teaches that knowledge is to know three categories of real things: souls, material nature and God [13.2–3]. Illusion arises when we mix up these three, mistaking one for the other.

Thus at times we think that souls are material, identifying ourselves with the body [15.8–10]; or we may vainly think *ourselves* God, or at least the lord of all we survey [16.14]; or we may think that God is material, or that He descends in a material body like ours [7.13, 7.24]; or we may think the total material universe to be supreme, with no God above it [16.8]. All these fundamental category mistakes cover our pure, transparent consciousness and separate us from our eternal, joyful life.

But one who knows categorically (*tattvataḥ*) Kṛṣṇa's divine birth and actions, does not take birth again, but goes to Kṛṣṇa for eternal life [4.9]. Knowledge of Kṛṣṇa's divine birth saves one from a mundane birth. Similarly, one who knows that *karma* does not bind Kṛṣṇa is also not bound by *karma* [4.14].

One who knows Kṛṣṇa as the great Lord of the worlds is liberated from all sins [10.3]. Knowing this knowledge of Kṛṣṇa, all the great sages achieved perfection; relying on this same knowledge, one achieves Kṛṣṇa's own nature [14.1–2]. One who teaches this knowledge of *Gītā* to the devoted achieves Kṛṣṇa [18.68]. And one who merely hears it with faith, without envy, is liberated and attains the holy worlds [18.71].

A *bhakti-yogī* cultivates pure love for God with deep knowledge, not blind sentiment. Thus Kṛṣṇa states that four kinds of people approach God: the suffering, the curious, those seeking prosperity, and one with true knowledge of God [7.16]. Of these, the one with knowledge has singular devotion, for Kṛṣṇa is exceedingly dear to those who truly know Him, and they are dear to Him [7.17]. Indeed one who knows Kṛṣṇa, and who always stands by Him, is like the Lord's very self [7.18]. That knower surrenders fully to God [7.19]. Clearly knowledge plays a vital role in true spiritual devotion: to know Kṛṣṇa is to love Him.

If Kṛṣṇa consciousness is so simple and sublime, why do so many people not know Kṛṣṇa? Recall Kṛṣṇa's statement that one is liberated by hearing Him with faith and *without envy* [18.71]. Kṛṣṇa elsewhere links faith (or trust) to non-envy: those who always follow His teaching, *trusting and not envying*, are freed from *karma* [3.31]. Similarly, He will teach this liberating knowledge to Arjuna because Arjuna does not envy God [9.1]. The demonic, however, despise and envy God, who dwells in their own and others' bodies [16.18]. The *Gītā* is not to be spoken to one who envies Kṛṣṇa [18.67]. On the other hand, one who trusts Kṛṣṇa achieves knowledge [4.39].

How do we explain this vital link between non-envy and knowledge? From within our hearts, Kṛṣṇa gives us either knowledge or ignorance [15.15] in fair reciprocation with our attitude toward Him [4.11, 9.29]. Some people simply do not like the idea of a Supreme Person, who is the Lord [16.8], and to these Kṛṣṇa presents the Godless world they desire. In other words, He respects our free will. Kṛṣṇa does not force Himself upon us, and thus we have the freedom to act on our envy and not believe in God. When we eventually tire of meaninglessness, Kṛṣṇa shows us life's true purpose.

Ultimately each of us elevates or degrades *ourselves*: self alone is self's friend or enemy; it is our choice [6.5–6]. Thus, near the *Gītā*'s end, Kṛṣṇa tells Arjuna to carefully consider all He has taught and then do as he wishes [18.63].

Finally Kṛṣṇa asks Arjuna if he has heard the message with single-pointed attention, and if his illusion, born of ignorance, is dispelled [18.72]. Arjuna replies that, by Kṛṣṇa's grace, his illusion is gone, his memory restored. He now stands firm and will execute Kṛṣṇa's instruction [18.73]. These are the last words spoken by Arjuna and Kṛṣṇa in *Bhagavad-gītā*.

Kṛṣṇa chose Arjuna to hear the *Gītā* precisely because Arjuna is the Lord's devoted friend [4.3]. For millennia Kṛṣṇa's devotees have accepted that to grasp the *Gītā* truly and deeply, and reap its rich spiritual rewards, one must follow Arjuna, the *Gītā*'s exemplary student. What does it mean, then, to practice *bhakti-yoga*, and thus follow the path of the great Arjuna?

How to Attain Kṛṣṇa

We naturally praise that which is truly great in beauty, power, kindness and wisdom. Thus throughout the world people have praised God in song, dance and prayer, and we also find this timeless process in *bhakti-yoga*.

Thus Arjuna says that upon hearing the Lord's glories, the world rejoices and embraces its Maker, and that this is rightly done [11.36]. Great souls, fixed in devotional vows, are always praising God, and bowing to Him with devotion [9.14]. They dwell in Kṛṣṇa [12.8], and thus have no deep sense of a material home in this world [12.19].

In offering a leaf, flower, fruit or water to Kṛṣṇa, the devoted truly offer their very self to Kṛṣṇa,[7] for their hearts go with their offering [9.26].

As explained earlier, the words *bhakti* (devotion) and *bhakta* (devotee) spring from the Sanskrit verb *bhaj*: to serve, honor, revere, love, adore. The *Gītā* often uses this verb to

---

[7] Kṛṣṇa says that one who offers with devotion, *bhaktyā prayacchati*, actually offers one's very soul, *prayata-ātmanaḥ* [9.26].

describe the Lord's devotees. In the following examples, the word *adore* always translates from the Sanskrit verb *bhaj*:

One who *adores* Kṛṣṇa, situated in all beings, is a real *yogī* who abides in Kṛṣṇa [6.31].

The highest *yogī adores* Kṛṣṇa with faith [6.47].

Even those who *adore* Kṛṣṇa with material motives are doing good [7.16].

Those free of duality *adore* Kṛṣṇa with firm vows [7.28].

Great souls *adore* Kṛṣṇa, knowing Him to be the eternal origin of all beings [9.13].

Kṛṣṇa abides in those who *adore* Him with devotion [9.29].

Having come to a temporary, unhappy world, *adore* the Lord [9.33]!

Realizing that Kṛṣṇa is the source of all, the wise *adore* Him [10.8].

Kṛṣṇa illumines the path to liberation for those who *adore* Him with love [10.10].

One who knows Kṛṣṇa as the Ultimate Person knows everything, and *adores* Him with all one's being [15.19].

This last verse warrants close attention: true *bhakti* means to offer all we do to Kṛṣṇa [9.27], to adore Him with all our being [15.19]. This requires serious spiritual practice. Thus a devotee should engage in *bhakti-yoga* without deviation [13.11, 14.26], for one attains the divine Supreme Person by *bhakti*, devotion, but also by the force of spiritual practice, *yoga* [8.11]. Kṛṣṇa's dear devotee is *always a yogī*, a serious spiritual practitioner [12.14].

Thus those who transcend sin, and whose deeds are pious, who are freed from duality-illusion, adore Kṛṣṇa with firm vows [7.28]. Kṛṣṇa emphasizes that His dear devotee transcends all sorts of duality, and so does not exult or hate, grieve or hanker, cling to weal or woe, etc. [12.17–19].

Kṛṣṇa is above nature's three modes,[8] and to find Kṛṣṇa, one must rise above these modes, which seduce us into material attraction and repulsion. Indeed nature's modes—goodness, passion and darkness—bewilder the whole world, hiding God from our view [7.13]. It is hard to surmount this divine illusory energy, *māyā*,[9] but those who surrender to Kṛṣṇa cross over His illusory energy [7.14].

Later, in a discussion on nature's modes, Arjuna asks Kṛṣṇa how one can transcend all three qualities and attain transcendence [14.21]. After describing the character and consciousness of a transcendent soul, Kṛṣṇa concludes that by serving God with undeviating *bhakti-yoga*, one fully transcends nature's qualities and achieves spiritual existence [14.26].

Those advanced in any field naturally associate with others advanced in that field, be it music, sports, scholarship, martial arts, fine arts, politics or whatever. So Kṛṣṇa teaches that His devotees naturally associate with and encourage each other. Minds fixed on Kṛṣṇa, they enlighten one another, always speaking of Kṛṣṇa, filling their lives with joy and satisfaction [10.9]. Indeed, one who teaches *Bhagavad-gītā* to Kṛṣṇa's devotees performs the highest act of devotion and will surely attain Kṛṣṇa [18.68].

Kṛṣṇa does not want His loving devotees to become entangled in mundane affairs and recommends that they remain aloof, *udāsīna* [12.16], just as He does [9.9]. In fact, this stoic detachment from passionate concerns takes one beyond the agitations of nature's modes [14.23].

Kṛṣṇa repeatedly offers to protect and shelter those who seek refuge in Him. The bewildered do not approach Kṛṣṇa, preferring the "shelter" of godless existence [7.15] or insatiable

---

[8] 4.14, 7.13, 13.15, 13.32, 14.19.

[9] Kṛṣṇa also speaks directly of *māyā*, His power of illusion, at 7.25 and 18.61; and at 4.6 He mentions His spiritual *ātma-māyā*, by which He descends to this world.

lust [16.10]—or of endless worries that end only with death [16.11]. Indeed those who ignore Kṛṣṇa's teachings effectively take shelter in their own egotism [18.59]. However, many souls have taken shelter of Kṛṣṇa and attained His nature [4.10]. Thus, ultimately, a wise person should depend neither on action's fruits [6.1] nor on any other being [3.18]. One should find shelter (*āśraya*) in Kṛṣṇa alone, as the *Gītā* repeatedly recommends:

We can know Kṛṣṇa if we practice spiritual life at His *shelter* [7.1].

Those striving for freedom from old age and death find *shelter* in Kṛṣṇa [7.29].

Even those of troublesome birth travel the highest path when they take *shelter* of Kṛṣṇa [9.32].

Those unable to strictly practice spiritual life find *shelter* in Kṛṣṇa by working on His behalf [12.11].

Performing all one's actions for Kṛṣṇa and *sheltered* in Him, by His mercy one attains the everlasting, unperishing place [18.56].

Moreover, *Kṛṣṇa is shelter (śaraṇam)* [9.18], and He urges us to go only to Him for *shelter (śaraṇam)* with all our being, so that by His mercy we attain highest peace and eternal abode [18.62]. Finally, in the *Gītā*'s famous climax, Kṛṣṇa urges Arjuna to give up his reliance on all other *dharmas* or duties, and come to Him alone for *shelter (śaraṇam)*, saying: "I will free you from all evils; do not worry" [18.66].

There are also times in which Kṛṣṇa advises Arjuna to rely on *Kṛṣṇa-related* shelters:

Great souls take *shelter* of the divine nature [9.13].

Those who take *shelter* of the knowledge Kṛṣṇa teaches attain His own nature [14.2].

One should seek *shelter* in *buddhi*, spiritual intelligence [2.49], which Kṛṣṇa awards to the devoted [10.10].

Taking *shelter* of this practical spiritual reason (*buddhi-yoga*), one should always think of Kṛṣṇa [18.57].

Kṛṣṇa personally satisfies all the needs of those who always think of Him, and are thus always linked to Him [9.22]. He promises Arjuna that His devotee never perishes [9.31]. For those who always meditate on Kṛṣṇa and dedicate all their deeds to Him, He personally and promptly uplifts them from the *death-wandering-ocean* [12.6–7]—the vast material world wherein souls wander through mortal bodies.

Kṛṣṇa fairly reciprocates with everyone; however we approach Him, He responds accordingly [4.11]. Kṛṣṇa is equal to all beings, neither favoring nor hating anyone. Yet He abides in those who devotedly abide in Him. Thus we attain the unique and supreme benefits of *bhakti-yoga* in proportion to our devotion. Kṛṣṇa makes clear that the goal is constant pure love, often speaking of *constancy* and *purity* when describing what devotion should be.

Constancy in Devotional Practice

Kṛṣṇa asks us to devote all that we do to Him [9.27], and six times He encourages us to be *always linked (engaged)* in devotional practice, or praises those that already are:

Of the four kinds of *good-doers* who approach God, best is the one with knowledge and singular devotion who is *always linked* [7.17]:

Kṛṣṇa is easy to attain for an *ever-engaged yogī* who remembers Him *constantly* [8.14].

Those who are firm in their devotional vows *continually* glorify the Lord and strive with devotion, *always engaged* [9.14].

Kṛṣṇa personally supplies the needs of those who are *always engaged* in their devotional practices [9.22].

Kṛṣṇa gives liberating spiritual intelligence to those *always engaged* in their devotional practice [10.10].

The best *yogīs* are *always engaged* in their devotional practice [12.2].

One should note that the word translated as *engaged* or *linked* is *yukta*, derived from the same root as *yoga*. Thus, if *yoga* means *link*, *yukta* means *linked*. In other words, to be always *yukta* is to be always immersed in one's spiritual practice, *yoga*.

Kṛṣṇa consistently states that one who *always* follows His teachings with faith and without envy is liberated from all *karma* [3.31]. Also, the wise find satisfaction and joy by *always* talking about Kṛṣṇa [10.9]. His dear devotee is *always* a satisfied *yogī* [12.14]. Thus Kṛṣṇa urges us to *always* fix our minds in Him [18.57].

Purity In Devotional Practice

The Sanskrit word *anya* means *other*, or *another*. The negative *an-anya* thus means *no other*, *sole* or *exclusive*. Kṛṣṇa uses this word *an-anya* eight times in the *Gītā*, and always to describe the pure, unadulterated nature of *bhakti* or *bhakti-yoga*:

Kṛṣṇa is easy to attain for those who always remember Him with their minds on *no other* [8.14].

Great souls adore Kṛṣṇa with their minds on *no other* [9.13].

Kṛṣṇa satisfies all the needs of those who are thinking of *no other* [9.22].

One can attain the Supreme Person by *bhakti* (devotion) that has *no other* object [8.22].

One is able to know, to see and to approach Kṛṣṇa in truth by *bhakti* that has *no other* object [11.54].

Even a person of very bad behavior can be thoroughly rectified by adoring Kṛṣṇa with *no other* object [9.30].

Kṛṣṇa personally saves from the material ocean those devoted to Him with *yoga* that has absolutely *no other* object [12.6].

True knowledge entails undeviating *bhakti* accompanied by *yoga* that has *no other* object [13.11].

We should here note that this is hardly a sectarian state of mind since everything exists in Kṛṣṇa and Kṛṣṇa exists in everything [6.30]—and since, in a sense, Kṛṣṇa *is* everything [7.19, 11.40]. The point is clear: Kṛṣṇa contains all that exists, and pure loving devotion to Kṛṣṇa includes the benefits of all other spiritual processes.

Thus, as our well-wishing friend [5.29], Kṛṣṇa urges us to devote ourselves to Him [9.34, 9.33, 18.65]. He assures Arjuna that the battle is already won by His grace, and that Arjuna should simply be the Lord's instrument [11.33].

History shows that, in the name of God, many people have harmed other people, as well as Earth itself. Do the *Gītā*'s teachings leave theological room for one to harm the innocent in Kṛṣṇa's name? Fortunately, not!

Compassion Toward All Beings

As we devote our actions to God, the higher taste of devotion gradually detaches us from nature's modes. An essential symptom of progress on this path is real concern for all God's creatures. Though aloof from mundane affairs, Kṛṣṇa's devotee cares very much about the ultimate wellbeing of all souls.

Kṛṣṇa states twice that one who is truly devoted to Him is also devoted to the welfare of *all* beings [5.25, 12.4]. The wise soul is not a mere *humanist*, but rather a merciful friend to all [12.13].

Kṛṣṇa speaks of Himself as the world's Father *and* Mother [9.17, 14.4]. Just as parents love their children equally, regardless of varying degrees of material talent, so Kṛṣṇa is equal to all souls [9.29, 13.28]—and expects His devotees to be the same [18.54]. This equality entails universal benevolence and beneficence, wishing and doing good to all. For Kṛṣṇa Himself is kind to all beings [5.29], seeing the ultimate equality of all souls [5.18, 18.54].

Kṛṣṇa's devotee does not disturb others [12.15] and does not hate any being [11.55, 12.13]. Both wisdom and austerity require *ahiṁsā*, never injuring or doing harm [13.8, 17.14]. Only those in nature's darkest modes engage in harmful, violent acts [18.25, 18.27].

Here we must keep in mind that the Sanskrit word *ahiṁsā* specifically refers to doing no *malicious* harm. Thus, in affirming *ahiṁsā*, Kṛṣṇa does not hypocritically praise non-violence on the one hand and urge Arjuna to fight against innocent non-combatants on the other. Rather He and Arjuna together are restoring justice to the world and protecting the innocent [2.31–33].

The demonic, however, perform horrible deeds against the world's welfare [16.9]. Those in darkness undergo austerities to defeat and ruin others [17.19]. True spirituality entails mercy toward all beings [16.2]. Kṛṣṇa personally comes to this world to defend and revive justice (*dharma*) and to save the virtuous [4.8].

We next explore *bhakti-yoga* as the highest form of *yajña* (offering to our divine source), which is itself the only way to escape the bondage of *karma* [3.9].

The Offering of Pure Love

Yajña, offering, inspires all the *Gītā*'s *yoga*s or spiritual paths. As the highest *yoga*, *bhakti-yoga* naturally constitutes the supreme offering. I will explain.

Better than a mere offering of material goods is the offering of one's open mind to spiritual truth: the knowledge-offering (*jñāna-yajña*) [4.33]. One performs this knowledge-offering by learning from the wise [4.34], and the knowledge thus gained is that all beings exist within the Supreme Soul, Kṛṣṇa [4.35].

We are eternal parts of Kṛṣṇa [15.7], and thus we nourish our own existence by offering to Him [15.7]. The part naturally serves the whole, just as the hand-part of the body naturally feeds itself by giving food to the stomach. Similarly, we water the whole tree by watering its root, and Kṛṣṇa is the root of all existence. Thus by serving Kṛṣṇa we best serve ourselves and all souls—or by nourishing our eternal link (*yoga*) with God, we best nourish ourselves and all souls.[10]

We thus attain highest truth by offering mind and reason to Kṛṣṇa [8.7, 12.14], for mind and reason are ultimately Kṛṣṇa's own energy [7.4]. Again, this does not mean that we lose our mind and reason; rather it means that we purify and enlighten them instead. To understand spiritual offering is to know that all we offer comes back to us exalted and immortalized, leading us to the Absolute [4.30]. Kṛṣṇa is the source of all [10.8], the Supreme Being upon whom the universe is woven [7.8].

The intimate link between the highest forms of *yoga* and *yajña* clearly emerges in two very similar verses, wherein Kṛṣṇa says: "Be mindful of Me, devoted to Me, offer to Me, bow to Me; thus linking your soul, fully devoted to Me, you will come to Me alone . . . I promise you this truly, for I love you" [9.34, 18.65]. And another in which He states: "one who offers to Me, comes to Me" [9.25].

Indeed, one attains peace by knowing that Kṛṣṇa is the *enjoyer* [5.29]. After describing the futility of offering to gods, which gains one only temporary rewards [9.20–21], Kṛṣṇa states that He personally brings all needed gifts to those who come to Him [9.22], that those who offer to gods are actually offering

---

[10] The *Bhāgavata-purāṇa* makes these points at 4.31.14: *Yathā taror mūla niṣecanena tṛpyanti tat-skandha-bhujopaśākhā, prāṇopahārāt yathendriyānam tathaiva sarvārhanam acyutejyā.*

to God, but indirectly and irregularly [9.23], and that He is the actual enjoyer and Lord of all offerings [9.24].

Karma-yoga, *jñāna-yoga* and *dhyāna-yoga* involve, respectively, engaging one's actions, studies and meditation in disciplined spiritual practice. On each path, by offering one's practice to the Divine, one completes the cosmic cycle of receiving and giving back, and thus one becomes a good cosmic citizen, a civilized soul. *Bhakti-yoga*, the path of offering pure love, includes and engages actions, studies and meditation, raising them to their purest spiritual pitch by infusing each activity with pure love of God and all God's creatures. In thus transforming one's life into a continuous spiritual offering, *bhakti-yoga* emerges as the highest of spiritual *yoga*s.

Kṛṣṇa describes *bhakti-yoga* as a spiritual offering of all of life to life's source: "All that you do, all that you eat, all that you sacrifice or give in charity, all austerity that you undertake, make that an offering to Me" [9.27]. In this verse, the word *offering* translates *arpaṇa*, the same key term Kṛṣṇa used at 4.24 in describing how *yajña* (offering) spiritualizes the one who offers and all that is offered. Thus in *bhakti-yoga*, one offers, and thus spiritualizes, all of one's life, clearing one's path to highest liberation in Kṛṣṇa, as we shall discuss in the next section. For now, here is a simple example of how *bhakti-yoga* works in practice as a pure offering.

Inspired by Kṛṣṇa's claim that He will accept even a leaf, a flower, fruit or water if offered with *bhakti* (devotion), we proceed to offer an apple to Kṛṣṇa with a simple bow and prayer. Let us first admit that it is *we* who are hungry, not Kṛṣṇa—*we* want the apple. But we've learned from *Bhagavad-gītā* that the apple is *ultimately* not an apple at all. It is pure energy briefly shaped into apple form, complete with taste and nutrients [13.20]. That pure energy, now appearing as an apple, emanates from Kṛṣṇa [10.8].

By conventional analysis, seed, earth, rain and sun produce the apple tree. Let us go down this list: Kṛṣṇa is the *perpetual seed* of all creatures, including apple trees [7.10, 9.18, 10.39, 14.4]. A seed needs soil, and *earth* also comes from Kṛṣṇa [7.4]. A seed in soil needs *rain* and Kṛṣṇa holds back and releases rain [9.19]. Now we just need *sunshine*, and that is also Kṛṣṇa [7.8].

You can guess the rest: the body that eats the apple is also Kṛṣṇa's energy; we souls merely witness the body's senses, touch and taste, interacting with their object, the apple [5.8–9]. Souls are Kṛṣṇa's superior energy [7.5]. Thus He is the life of our life [7.9], for we are part of Him [15.7].

Considering all the above, offering Kṛṣṇa the fruit of our work, in this case an apple, with a friendly bow and a word of gratitude, and thus inviting Him to enjoy the apple before we do, is the least we can do. We must distinguish *yajña*, offering, from *dāna*, charity or giving to someone in need. Kṛṣṇa does not need our apple, but we need to purify our soul by learning gratitude and devotion. The more our offering is truly devoted, and not perfunctory or mechanical, the more we advance spiritually.

When Kṛṣṇa accepts our offering, His spiritual power spiritualizes the apple [4.24], transforming it into *yajña-śiṣṭa*, a sacrificial remnant [3.13, 4.30]. Eating that apple, we spiritualize our body and make it an ally in our journey to liberation. We are freed from past offenses (bad *karma*) and achieve true spiritual existence [4.30].

Devotion is key. When our love for God grows so strong that we want Kṛṣṇa to enjoy the apple more than we want to enjoy it ourselves, then we are acting as pure souls and our actions accrue no material *karma*. We act for God, not ourselves. We eat to keep our body healthy so that we may serve the One we love. This devoted active love is called *bhakti*. The *Gītā* assures us that when we act for God (*yajña*) our *karma* entirely dissolves [4.23].

This same principle holds true for every other spiritual path that Kṛṣṇa teaches. A *karma-yogī* devotes his or her natural vocation to Kṛṣṇa. But just as, at first, one piously offers the apple to God, yet mainly wants it for oneself, so in the beginning, one piously offers one's vocation to God, but is mainly attached to the worldly work of a teacher, ruler, proprietor or worker. As one grows spiritually, one's devotion for Kṛṣṇa surpasses one's attachment to career. One stays in one's profession but attachment shifts to God. Similarly, the pious scholar or philosopher gradually learns to love Kṛṣṇa even more than his or her own prodigious intellect; and the meditator outgrows attachment to power over the body and mystic visions, and falls in love with Kṛṣṇa.

To conclude with our apple analogy, planting an apple seed, watering it, harvesting the apples, cleaning and slicing them, etc.—all these acts rise to the spiritual platform when we perform them with devotion (*bhakti*), clearly seeing that they form part of our loving offering to God. Devotion is our natural link to God, and by offering Him an apple or any other material possession, we fulfill matter's ultimate purpose: to serve the infinitely benevolent will of its Maker.

Kṛṣṇa tells us to offer all that we do to Him. This is the essence of spiritual life in *bhakti-yoga* and in the *Gītā*—the perfection of life itself. For we are all eternal parts of Kṛṣṇa [15.7].

PART XII
Mukti (Liberation)

Negative Liberation (Freedom *from*)

Words like *free* and *freedom* have both a negative and a positive sense, with the negative indicating that one is free *from* unwanted restraint, control, slavery, subjugation, domination, etc., and the positive indicating that one is free *to* act and live as one wants.

Bhagavad-gītā speaks expansively about *freedom from* and *freedom to*, for Kṛṣṇa's goal is to liberate the soul. We will first consider the negative aspect of freedom and then the positive.

Most generally, Kṛṣṇa speaks of being *liberated* [4.32, 18.71], or *happily freed from bondage* [5.3], adding that *godly qualities conduce to liberation* [16.5]. More specifically, Kṛṣṇa speaks of being freed from nature's three modes [2.45, 14.20–26], and the term *guṇātīta*[1] is a synonym for *liberated.*

The *Gītā* also teaches freedom from attachment [3.9, 4.23, 18.26], and from the negative qualities attachment produces: lust and anger [5.26]; desire, fear and anger [5.28]; or the *three gateways* to darkness—lust, rage and greed [16.22].

Kṛṣṇa speaks about being freed from dualities such as attachment and aversion [2.65], hating and hankering [5.3], exulting, intolerance, fear and affliction [12.15], or joy and sorrow [15.5].

---

[1] *Guṇātīta* is derived from *guṇa* (quality/mode), *ati* (beyond), and *ita* (gone), literally "*gone beyond* [*material nature's*] *modes.*"

He also speaks generally of becoming duality-less, *nir-dvandva* [2.45, 5.3], of going beyond duality, *dvandvātīta* [4.22], and of being freed from duality-illusion, *dvandva-moha* [7.28].

Kṛṣṇa speaks of being freed from all misfortune, *aśubha*, and from all sins or offenses [3.13, 10.3]; and He personally frees from all sins those who come to Him alone for shelter [18.66].

The *Gītā* speaks of being liberated from *karma*-bondage [2.39, 3.21, 4.14], which manifests as the unavoidable fruit (or consequence) of our mundane actions [9.28]. Thus one can act in this world without binding reaction [4.22] and achieve perfect freedom from *karma* [18.49].

It is *karma* that obliges us to repeatedly take birth and die in this world, and so to be free of *karma* is to free oneself from the cycle of births and deaths. Since re-birth entails re-death, Kṛṣṇa abbreviates by speaking sometimes of freeing oneself from birth and sometimes of freeing oneself from death.

Thus, on the one hand, Kṛṣṇa describes liberation as *no rebirth* [4.9, 8.15, 8.16] and the liberated person as *one who does not take birth again* [13.24], or who is *freed from birth bondage* [2.51]. He also speaks of successful spiritualists as those who *go to non-return* [5.17, 8.26].

Yet again, Kṛṣṇa speaks of *one who qualifies for immortality* [2.15], and of those who, by various spiritual paths, *cross over death* [13.26], who successfully *seek liberation from old age and death* [7.29], and *who are freed from the miseries of birth, death and old age* [14.20].

We should clearly keep in mind that all those things *from which* we are to gain freedom—the problem of bondage, nature's three modes, attachment, anger, lust, greed, dualities, misfortune, sin, *karma*, birth, old age and death—are simply different facets of a single condition, which may be called *illusion*. Thus to be fully free of nature's modes is to be free of dualities, which is to be free of attachments, which is to be free of binding *karmic* action, which is to be free of birth, death, rebirth and again dying.

This then is the negative aspect of freedom—freedom *from*. What does the *Gītā* teach us about liberation's positive side? To what most desirable state does spiritual liberation lead?

Positive Liberation (Freedom *to*)

True freedom entails positive freedom to do all that is worthy, valuable and beneficial for ourselves and those we love. As we shall see, liberation is a state of mind, a type of action, and a place.

Peace (Śānti)

We begin this analysis of the *Gītā*'s statements on freedom's positive goals and rewards with a quality we can all appreciate: *śānti* (peace), freedom from unwanted disturbance, pain, frustration, sadness, etc. Here, as with other positive states and qualities, Kṛṣṇa will describe a virtuous but worldly as well as a more spiritual version of the same quality.

Kṛṣṇa makes some common sense observations about peace:

Without *peace*, where is happiness [2.66]?

One not disturbed by selfish desires that flow into the mind, attains *peace* [2.70].

One who gives up possessiveness and egotism achieves *peace* [2.71].

Peace comes from letting go [12.12].

Kṛṣṇa also speaks of truly spiritual peace, attained in an enlightened state:

Gaining knowledge, one soon achieves *supreme peace* [4.38].

Giving up fruits of action, a linked practitioner attains *final peace* [5.12].

Knowing Kṛṣṇa, one finds *peace* [5.29].

The *yogī*, always linking self, achieves *nirvāṇa of highest peace*, which abides in Me [6.15].

A virtuous soul and devotee, rectified of bad conduct, attains *everlasting peace*, for My devotee never perishes [9.31].

Śānti, peace, is part of the divine nature [16.2].

One who goes to Kṛṣṇa alone for shelter, quickly attains *supreme peace* by Kṛṣṇa's grace [18.62].

Grace (Prasāda)

Related to *śānti*, peace, is a sublime state of mind called *prasāda*, which in the *Gītā* means a serene clarity of mind that puts one in a state of grace. Here too, we find both a basic and a more advanced use of the word.

Kṛṣṇa introduces the term in the second chapter, where He states that a self-controlled, accomplished soul achieves *prasāda*, serene clarity and grace [2.64]. In that state of *prasāda*, all miseries subside and reason (*buddhi*) quickly grows steady [2.65]. Further, mind-*prasāda*—keeping the mind clear, serene and in grace—is a mental austerity [17.16], since the mind often irrationally seeks more passionate states. And happiness in the material mode of goodness arises from serene clarity (*prasāda*) of self and reason [18.37]. Thus *prasāda* strengthens *buddhi*, and that serene reason produces virtuous joy.

Along with the noun *prasāda*, Kṛṣṇa uses the adjective *prasanna*, which describes one in a state of grace or clarity, and may also indicate a state of benevolence or graciousness toward another. Thus Kṛṣṇa describes Himself as *prasanna*, benevolently disposed, toward Arjuna, and so, willing to show Arjuna the Lord's personal form [11.47]. Also, a soul who has attained *brahman*, spiritual existence, becomes a *prasanna*-soul—a soul immersed in enlightening, calming grace, with nothing for which to hanker or lament [18.54].

Success, Perfection (Siddhi)

Kṛṣṇa often uses the word *siddhi*, which means *success, full attainment*, even *perfection* and *spiritual beatitude*. Kṛṣṇa also uses the form *sam-siddhi*, adding to *siddhi* the suffix *sam*, which here means *fully, intensely, completely*. Thus the word *saṁsiddhi* emphatically means *full* success, *complete* perfection, etc.

Kṛṣṇa certainly knows that some people truly aspire for spiritual perfection, whereas others seek only a type of worldly self-improvement. The word *siddhi* may apply to both, since to achieve one's virtuous, mundane goals is also a form of *siddhi*.

Thus those seeking *siddhi*, success in their worldly actions, make offerings to gods and quickly receive the *siddhi* they seek: material prosperity [4.12]. In general, one must pay attention to place, agent, instrument, effort and providence to achieve *siddhi*, success in any action, be it proper or improper [18.14–15].

The word *siddhi* may also refer to the mystic powers one obtains through advanced *yoga* practice. In that sense, the word *siddha*, meaning *perfected* or *accomplished*, may be applied to *yogīs*, sages or celestial beings that perfect these or other higher powers. Thus in the *identity verses* of Chapter Ten, Kṛṣṇa says that among *siddhas*, perfected beings, He is the divine sage Kapila [10.26].

Within Kṛṣṇa's cosmic form, Arjuna sees societies of great sages and *siddhas*, perfected beings, entering the Lord's all-devouring form [11.21]; celestial *Siddhas* all gaze astonished upon the Lord [11.22]; and all accomplished (*siddha*) societies bow to the Lord upon hearing His glories [11.36].

Kṛṣṇa teaches the best knowledge, knowing which all great sages attained the highest perfection (*siddhi*) [14.1].

By thorough detachment, self-control and renunciation one attains the perfection (*siddhi*) of freedom from *karma* [18.49]. Kṛṣṇa explains how one attains that perfection: ultimately one must devote oneself to Kṛṣṇa [18.50–54].

However, Kṛṣṇa warns us that not all who seek or attain a particular perfection can understand Him. In fact, among thousands of human beings, one may actually seek perfection (*siddhi*), and of those who strive and achieve their preferred perfection, only a rare soul will understand Kṛṣṇa in truth [7.3].

Kṛṣṇa gives these examples of spiritual *siddhi*:

Kṛṣṇa teaches that each member of society can attain full perfection (*saṁsiddhi*) by performing his or her respective duties in a mood of worshiping the Lord [18.45–46]. King Janaka and other saintly rulers attained full perfection (*saṁsiddhi*) precisely in this way, by simply performing their duties in *karma-yoga* [3.20].

One fully perfected in *yoga* (*yoga-saṁsiddhi*) discovers most purifying wisdom [4.38].

Kṛṣṇa explains how sincere *yogīs* achieve full perfection (*saṁsiddhi*) even if it takes them several lives [6.40–45], and the highest stage of such successful *yoga* is to adore Kṛṣṇa [6.47].

Performing one's actions for Kṛṣṇa's sake, one achieves perfection (*siddhi*) [12.10].

A word of caution: one who rejects sacred-wisdom texts like *Bhagavad-gītā* cannot achieve perfection (*siddhi*) [16.23], but rather remains enmeshed in nature's modes [17.1–2].

Purification (Śuddhi, Pavitra)

Kṛṣṇa teaches us to practice *yoga* for *self-purification* [5.11, 6.12], for a purified soul, through perfect empathy, becomes the very soul of all beings, and is not tainted by actions [5.7]. Living purely is a divine asset [16.3], and keeping one's life pure requires mental discipline or austerity [17.16]. A *yogī* attains full success only when fully purified of sins [6.45]. One also needs purified reason to attain true spiritual life [18.51].

In all the above verses, Kṛṣṇa uses various forms of the verb *śudh*, "to purify or be purified," such as *śuddhi* (purification or purity), *saṁśuddhi* (full purification or purity), *viśuddha* (purified), etc.

The *Gītā* also uses the word *pavitram*, purifier, four times as follows:

There is no purifier like spiritual knowledge [4.38]. Thus Kṛṣṇa's teachings are the ultimate purifier [9.2]. Kṛṣṇa is Himself the purifier [9.17], for He is knowledge [13.18] and the source of knowledge [15.15]. Indeed, as Arjuna states, Kṛṣṇa is the *supreme purifier* [10.12].

To purify is to remove impurities—i.e., to remove all that is foreign, harmful, debasing, contaminating or objectionable. The very notion of purifying an object indicates that the object possesses a pure, retrievable state.

Thus to speak of purifying the soul is to indicate that the soul has an original pure nature. Spiritual liberation, therefore, is to free the soul from all that is not the pure self.

Kṛṣṇa also explains this another way: lust and anger *cover* the soul, just as smoke covers fire, dust covers a mirror, or the womb covers the embryo [3.37–38]. Thus our perpetual enemy, lust, *covers* our awareness [3.39]. Lust, or selfish desire, infects our senses, mind and reason, confusing us by *covering* our awareness [3.40].

Similarly, ignorance (*un-knowledge* in Sanskrit) *covers* our knowledge and bewilders us [5.15]. Kṛṣṇa *conceals* or *covers* Himself from our view by His *yoga-māyā*, His power of mystic illusion; thus we do not recognize Him [7.25]. When we are careless, mistaken or mad, darkness *covers* our knowledge [14.9]. And spiritual reason goes dark when it is *covered* by nature's mode of darkness [18.32].

These many references to *covered* knowledge match the image of purification. We all possess perfect knowledge of God. We simply must uncover (discover) it. We do this by purifying our existence through spiritual practice (*yoga*), removing from our minds and hearts all that is not true and pure. What remains is pristine, crystalline awareness of reality: souls, nature and God.

When we discover who we really are, we naturally discover our real home. As eternal beings, we have an eternal abode, as explained throughout *Bhagavad-gītā*. But what is that everlasting home? How does *Bhagavad-gītā* describe it?

Brahman, the Supreme Imperishable

In *Bhagavad-gītā*, Kṛṣṇa teaches that *brahman* (spirit), the supreme imperishable, is both a spiritual destination and a spiritual state of being for souls; *brahman* is eternal and personal, its nature being Higher Self [8.3]. This is the primary meaning of *brahman* in the *Gītā*, but let us quickly review other meanings. Kṛṣṇa twice calls the total material energy *brahman* [14.3–4],[2] since *He* is its source [10.8] and *it* is His separated nature [7.4]. Kṛṣṇa also refers to Vedic scripture as *brahman* [3.15, 6.44]—a normal, if not primary, usage. And He twice calls the sacred syllable *Om*, *brahman* [8.13, 17.23].

However, He mainly uses the term *brahman* in its most celebrated and important sense, as found in the *Upaniṣads*,[3] the *knowledge-portion* of the Vedas. Therein *brahman* primarily refers to the pure, eternal existence shared by God and souls.

---

[2] The great *Vedānta* commentator Rāmānuja points out in his commentary to *Gītā* 14.3 that even older *Śruti* literature sometimes designates material nature as *brahman*: *śrutāv api kvacit prakṛtir api brahma iti nirdiśyate.*

[3] The *Upaniṣads* are the Vedic tradition's body of philosophical and theological texts, some very ancient, others less so.

For well over a millennium, sophisticated Indian theologians have argued and speculated about the precise meaning of *brahman* in the *Upaniṣads*, as have Western scholars and mystics over the last few centuries. Some have claimed that an impersonal monistic *brahman* is the highest truth, into which liberated souls *merge*, shedding individual identity and personality. And since Kṛṣṇa speaks of *brahman* in the *Gītā*, some have argued that Kṛṣṇa advocates this sort of impersonal liberation into absolute oneness. However, a careful review of what the *Gītā* actually says about *brahman* gives a very different picture. Let us begin.

Brahman, spiritual being, stands above nature's three modes [14.26], beyond death [4.30, 7.29, 13.13, 14.27]. Further, it brings exquisite, unlimited spiritual pleasure. Thus full contact with *brahman* joyfully brings unending joy [6.28] and pleasure without limits. But to find that endless *inner* pleasure, one engaged in *brahma-yoga* must not cling to *external* contacts [5.21], produced by contact of senses with their objects. And to relish that unperishing pleasure, one must also know that *brahman* is subordinate to Kṛṣṇa [13.13], for He is the *Supreme Brahman* [10.12], the foundation of immortal, unperishing *brahman*, and the source of absolute pleasure [14.27].

Kṛṣṇa further declares that one fully knows *brahman* by taking shelter of Him [7.29]. Hearing this, Arjuna at once asks, "what is this *brahman*" [8.1]. Kṛṣṇa replies that Brahman is the supreme imperishable, and its nature is *Higher Self* [8.3]. Again, *brahman* is not impersonal, for its nature is an individual self.

Kṛṣṇa twice declares that a soul may qualify for or partake of *brahman* existence (*brahma bhūyāya kalpate*). In both cases, the soul achieves *brahman* not by declaring to be God, but rather by devotion to God, Kṛṣṇa, who is both the basis of *brahman* [14.27] and the Supreme *Brahman* Himself [10.12].

Here are the two cases: one who serves the Lord with undeviating *bhakti-yoga* fully transcends nature's modes and thus qualifies for *brahman* existence [14.26]; similarly, one who assiduously practices spiritual life, qualifies for *brahman* existence and attains supreme devotion to Kṛṣṇa in that *brahman* state [18.54].

Three times Kṛṣṇa describes a soul who has come to exist as *brahman* (*brahma-bhūta*): A *yogī* with inner joy, inner delight and real inner light exists as *brahman* [5.24]. Yet even this *yogī* attains peace by realizing that God is the great Lord of all worlds and the dear friend of all beings [5.29]. Ultimate joy comes to a sinless *yogī* of calmed mind and quieted passion, who has come to exist as *brahman* [6.27]. This process leads to seeing Kṛṣṇa in all beings and all beings in Kṛṣṇa [6.29–31], for *yoga* culminates in devotion to Kṛṣṇa [6.47]. Indeed the *brahma-bhūta yogī* is one who finds pleasure and light within, and it is Kṛṣṇa Himself who dwells within the *yogī's* heart [6.47, 15.15, 18.61].

Lastly, one who has come to exist as *brahman* is equal to all beings and attains supreme devotion to Kṛṣṇa [18.54]. Thus devotion to Kṛṣṇa is not a stepping-stone to merging into an impersonal reality. Rather, it is precisely on the *brahman* platform that one finally attains pure love of God.

Five times Kṛṣṇa gives *nirvāṇa* as a spiritual goal, and the first four instances qualify it as *brahma-nirvāṇa*. The Sanskrit term *nirvāṇa* is grammatically negative since *nir-vāṇa* means without-*vāṇa*. The word *vāna*, from the root *vā*, means *blowing (of wind, tide or fire)*. Thus *nir-vāṇa*, both here and in Buddhism, traditionally means to end the gusting of material desire and rebirth, to extinguish the fire of selfish desire, to stop the tide of reincarnation, etc. In the literal sense of *nirvāṇa*, one seeks freedom *from* the undesirable tide of birth and death. The word *nir-vāṇa*, by itself, does not specify a positive state beyond *vāna*. Thus Kṛṣṇa's term *brahma-nirvāṇa* adds the supremely positive element *brahman* to the eliminating process of *nirvāṇa*. Positive awareness of *brahman* extinguishes the material fire, for one stops (*nir-*) the waves (*vāna*) of rebirth and realizes the Absolute (*brahman*). And to know *brahman* is to live in *brahman* [5.20].

Thus one is not only free *from* illusion, but also free *to* experience the highest joy in *brahman*.

Surely if Kṛṣṇa wanted to describe *brahman* as an impersonal goal, here is the opportunity, considering the non-personal term *brahma-nirvāṇa*, consisting of a neuter word, *brahman*, and a privative concept, *nir-vāna*. Yet here too, Kṛṣṇa mentions neither an impersonal destination for the soul nor a loss of personal identity.

To the contrary, *brahma-nirvāṇa* appears three times in Chapter Five [5.24–26], which ends with a ringing declaration of Kṛṣṇa's personal supremacy over all worlds [5.29]. *Brahma-nirvāṇa* also appears at the end of Chapter Two [2.72], after Kṛṣṇa has explicitly taught in that same chapter that He Himself and all souls exist eternally as individuals [2.12]. Lastly, to clarify that *nirvāṇa* also exists within God, Kṛṣṇa states in Chapter Six that the *nirvāṇa* of highest peace exists firmly within Him [6.15]. This chapter also ends by declaring the supremacy of *bhakti-yoga* [6.47], which rests on a personal, loving relationship between soul and God.

Kṛṣṇa stresses that one who achieves *brahma-nirvāṇa* cuts off biased duality and works for the welfare of all beings [5.25]. Thus *brahma-nirvāṇa* increases compassion and personal sensibility rather than extinguishing it. After all, upon seeing oneself as individual *brahman*, one sees every other being as equally *brahman*, for *brahman* is the true shared nature of every being. *Brahma-nirvāṇa* is not for those absorbed in liking or disliking other people's bodies. Rather, one who finds joy *within*, pleasure *within*, light *within*, attains *brahma-nirvāṇa*, and thus exists as *brahman* (pure spirit) even in this world [5.24]. Bodies differ; souls are equal. Thus *brahma-nirvāna* reveals and fosters deep unity among all beings.

Kṛṣṇa underlines the *flawless equality* of *brahman*. Thus to embrace the spiritual equality of all creatures is to stand in *brahman* [5.19]. Similarly, one who perceives that a state of spiritual unity underlies the diverse nature of all creatures, unites with expansive *brahman* [13.31]. One living as *brahman* is equal to all beings and attains supreme devotion to Kṛṣṇa, of Whom all beings are part [18.54].

Three times, Kṛṣṇa speaks of *going to brahman* [4.24, 4.30, 8.24], twice He speaks of *attaining brahman* [5.6, 18.50], and once each He speaks of *standing in brahman* [5.20] and *advancing to brahman* [13.31]. None of these descriptions explicitly reveal an impersonal or monist destination for the soul.

Twice Kṛṣṇa does speak literally of *oneness* (*ekatvam*). A *yogī* abiding in *oneness* worships Kṛṣṇa, who is present in all beings [6.31]. Here *oneness* does not merge soul and God into one being, but rather promotes the unity of all beings precisely because God is equally present in all of them.

The *bhakti-yogīs* always praise the Lord, endeavoring with firm vows, bowing to and worshiping God [9.14]. And yet others, offering with a knowledge-offering (*jñāna-yajña*), worship the Lord either in *oneness*, in *separateness* or in the *multi-form* facing everywhere [9.15]. Here *oneness* (*ekatvam*) refers to one of many options for worshiping God, not for becoming God. Indeed, all these options are located within *jñāna-yajña*, which, by definition, is an offering, *yajña*, from an inferior to a superior. Thus verse 9.15 does not espouse anything like monism, but rather reaffirms the soul's duty to worship God.

Kṛṣṇa states elsewhere that a soul *advances* to *brahman* (*brahma sampadyate*) by seeing that beings' distinct states *stand in one* [13.31]; Kṛṣṇa also often states that beings *stand* within *Him* [6.29, 6.30, 9.4, 9.6]. Again, the *One* is clearly Kṛṣṇa.

Reaching Kṛṣṇa

As explained earlier, the *Gītā* speaks of transcending death [2.15, 13.26], of being freed from the miseries of birth, death and old age and enjoying immortality [14.20], of being freed from birth bondage and going to *a place of no malady* [2.51], of going to *never-return* [5.17] or *non-return* [8.26] and of never taking birth again [13.24].

Though tantalizing, these spiritual options are still somewhat vague. What is immortality? What is *the place of no malady*, of *never-return*, etc.? To answer these vital questions, we must turn to a special set of *Gītā* verses that not only promise freedom from death and malady, but also speak more specifically about eternal life. These verses describe the soul's journey to Kṛṣṇa Himself:

One who understands Kṛṣṇa's divine birth and action does not take birth again, but rather goes to Kṛṣṇa [4.9].

Striving for freedom from old age and death, souls take shelter of Kṛṣṇa [7.29].

Reaching Kṛṣṇa, one does not take birth again in this temporary sad world, for one has gone to supreme and full perfection [8.15].

Reaching Kṛṣṇa, there is no more birth [8.16].

Reaching Kṛṣṇa's supreme abode, they never return [8.21].

Going to that place of the Original Person, they do not ever return [15.4].

Going to Kṛṣṇa's supreme abode, they do not return [15.6].

In these verses, the *Gītā* speaks of going to Kṛṣṇa, to the place where He lives, to His supreme abode. We will now consider in greater detail the language used to describe the soul's journey to Kṛṣṇa and His abode.

Padam

The Sanskrit word *padam* can mean a *place*, *site*, *abode* or *home*. This word first appears in the *Gītā* when Kṛṣṇa says that those freed of birth bondage go to the *place with no malady* [2.51].

Later Kṛṣṇa makes clear that this *padam*, or place, is His abode: one is to search for *that place*, going to which, they never return; there one surrenders to the Original Person [15.4]. Purified liberated souls go to that unperishing *place*; sun does not light it, nor moon, nor fire. Going there they never return, for that is Kṛṣṇa's supreme abode [15.6].

Near the *Gītā*'s end, Kṛṣṇa speaks one last time of that *padam* which is His supreme abode: those who specifically take shelter of Kṛṣṇa attain, by His mercy, that everlasting, unperishing *place* [18.56].

Sthānam

The Sanskrit *sthāna* (cognate with English *standing, state, status, station*, etc.) can mean *a continuous state of being, a place of staying*—and thus *a place, locality, abode, dwelling*, etc.

Kṛṣṇa teaches that the *yogī* who successfully departs this world reaches the *supreme, original sthāna*, or place [8.28]. Later Kṛṣṇa commands us to take shelter of Him alone, for thus, by His mercy, we will reach the everlasting *sthāna* [18.62]—i.e., His abode.

Paramāṁ gatim

Kṛṣṇa speaks five times of the *supreme destination*[4]—*parā* or *paramām gatim*—and makes very clear that one arrives there by devotion to Kṛṣṇa, for that supreme destination is His abode:

Steadily remembering Kṛṣṇa while quitting the body, one goes to that *supreme destination* [8.13].

[4] *Supreme destination*: in my *Gītā* translation (found herein), I sometimes translate *gati* as *way*, since it comes from the verb *gam*, "to go." However, verses like 8.21 make clear that *gati* here means not only a *way* or *path*, but also a place, specifically the place one goes to, a *destination*.

Beyond this nature is another nature that is eternal. When all creatures are perishing here, that higher world does not perish. They call it the *supreme destination*, and reaching it, they never return, for it is Kṛṣṇa's supreme abode [8.20–21].

Whoever takes shelter of Kṛṣṇa goes to the *supreme destination* [9.32].

Seeing the Lord situated equally everywhere, one does not harm oneself and goes to the *supreme destination* [13.29].

Freed from lust, anger and greed, the three gateways to darkness, one helps oneself and goes to the *supreme destination* [16.22].

By now, we know what that place is.

Dhāma

The primary sense of the Sanskrit word *dhāma* is *dwelling place, house, abode, domicile*. Kṛṣṇa and Arjuna, twice each, use *dhāma* in interesting ways.

Kṛṣṇa twice refers to "*that Supreme abode of Mine*" as follows (and as we saw above):

"Yet higher than this unmanifest is another eternal unmanifest, which does not perish when all beings are vanishing. They call that imperishable *unmanifest* the highest path, reaching which they do not return; for *that is My supreme abode*" [8.20–21].

"Sun does not light it, nor moon, nor fire. Going there, they do not return. *That is My supreme abode*" [15.6].

We see that Kṛṣṇa's supreme abode is self-luminous, and so attractive that once reaching it "they do not return."

Arjuna twice speaks of Kṛṣṇa's *supreme abode*, and both times declares that Kṛṣṇa *is* the supreme abode [10.12, 11.38]! Consonant with Arjuna's claim, Kṛṣṇa then tells him: "Fix your mind in Me alone, invest your reason in Me. You shall henceforth *dwell in Me alone*, no doubt" [12.8]. Thus Kṛṣṇa's abode is a spiritual extension of the Godhead. To know and love Kṛṣṇa is to dwell in Kṛṣṇa. The *Gītā* affirms the deeply personal nature of God and liberation. Those who reciprocate Kṛṣṇa's own pure love for them go to the eternal abode that is their real home.

Just as a loving parent yearns for a wayward child to come home, Kṛṣṇa makes clear that His own eternal world awaits us. Strikingly, at least sixteen times He explicitly explains how the soul, who is part of Kṛṣṇa, can "come to Me," "reach Me," etc.[5] Indeed, Kṛṣṇa assures us that if we simply remember Him always, and always engage in devotion, we can easily attain Him [8.14].

At the beginning of *Bhagavad-gītā*, Arjuna tried, but failed, to solve his own profound problems. He then accepted Kṛṣṇa as his teacher and declared to the Lord: "I am your disciple; teach me, for I am surrendered to you" [2.7].

The word *surrendered*, *prapanna*, comes from the root *pra-pad*, which literally means *to go forward* or *to approach*. In devotional Sanskrit literature like *Bhagavad-gītā* this verb *pra-pad* often means *to approach for shelter*—and in that sense, *to submit, surrender* or *devote oneself*.

Using this same verb, Kṛṣṇa explains the following:

He fairly reciprocates with all beings in the same way that they approach (*pra-pad*) Him [4.11].

Those whose knowledge is stolen by many material desires approach (*pra-pad*) other deities [7.14], meaning *gods* and not God.

Those who submit (*pra-pad*) to scriptures offering mundane rewards remain entangled in mortality [9.21].

---

[5] 4.9, 7.23, 8.7–8, 8.10, 9.25, 9.28, 9.34, 10.10, 11.55, 12.4, 12.9, 18.55, 18.65–66, 18.68.

Kṛṣṇa's divine illusory energy, *māyā*, is hard to overcome, but those who approach (*pra-pad*) Kṛṣṇa cross beyond it [7.14].

After many births, one with knowledge surrenders (*pra-pad*) to Kṛṣṇa, knowing that He is everything [7.19].

One should search for the place of the Original Person and therefore surrender (*pra-pad*) to Him [15.4].

Clearly, to do all this requires *faith*. Let us then look at the Sanskrit words for faith. From the word *asti*, "he, she or it exists," comes the word *āstikya*, faith that God exists [18.42]. But to indicate faith, Kṛṣṇa almost invariably uses the word *śraddhā*, which indicates not only a mental state of believing, but also a dynamic act of placing one's trust.[6] Let us see how Kṛṣṇa uses this word:

Those who always follow Kṛṣṇa's teaching with *faith* (*śraddhā*) are freed from all *karma* [3.31].

Those with *faith* (*śraddhā*) attain knowledge [4.39].

The best *yogīs* adore Kṛṣṇa with *faith* (*śraddhā*) [6.47].

Higher than impersonal mystics are those who worship Kṛṣṇa with transcendent *faith* (*śraddhā*) [12.2].

Those who honor Kṛṣṇa's immortal teachings, putting their *faith* (*śraddhā*) in them, are exceedingly dear to Kṛṣṇa [12.20].

Faith (*śraddhā*) arises in everyone, and those who do not accept sacred teachings will develop *faith* in nature's three modes and thus determine their existence materially [17.1–3].

A person willing to hear *Bhagavad-gītā* with *faith* (*śraddhā*), and without envy, can reach the beautiful worlds of those who perform holy deeds [18.71].

On the other hand, an unbelieving, unknowing person, a soul filled with doubts, is lost in this world and the next, and does not attain real happiness [4.40].

---

[6] *Śraddhā* is also a verb meaning to place (*dhā*) trust (*śrad*).

Those not believing in the *Gītā*'s path do not reach Kṛṣṇa. They return to the path of *death-wandering* [9.3]—i.e., the world of repeated birth and death.

An offering performed without *faith* is declared to be in darkness [17.13].

Without *faith*, whatever is offered or given or performed as austerity is said to be unreal, here and hereafter [17.28].

Mad-bhāva

Earlier in this work, I explained that God and souls are both one and different, as clearly expressed in the very language of the *Gītā*. Thus God and souls are both *puruṣa*, persons, but Kṛṣṇa is *parama puruṣa*, the Supreme Person, *uttama puruṣa*, the Ultimate Person, etc.

Kṛṣṇa is God, and yet throughout the *Gītā*, He reveals His unity with us by inviting us to come to "My state of being" (*mad-bhāva*) [4.10, 8.5, 13.9, 14.19].

In two very important verses, Kṛṣṇa speaks of those who do not understand His higher state of being or nature, *param bhāvam*.

The irrational, not knowing Kṛṣṇa's higher nature (*param bhāvam*), which is unperishing and supreme, believe that formless being takes on a visible personal form [7.24].[7]

---

[7] For Sanskritists, a few remarks on the verse: *avyaktaṁ vyaktim āpannam manyante mām abuddhayaḥ; param bhāvam ajānanto mamāvyayam anuttamam*. One might conjecture that either *avyaktam* or *vyaktim* might serve as the first object of *manyante*, with the remaining word being the object of *āpannam*. However, *āpannam* must be in apposition to *avyaktam*, since *vyaktim* is feminine and would thus produce *āpannām*, were those two words in apposition. So the meaning is: the irrational (*abuddhayaḥ*) believe (*manyante*) Me (*mām*) to be an *avyaktam* (unmanifest, impersonal being) who has taken on (*āpannam*) visible personal existence (*vyaktim*).

Similarly, the foolish, not knowing Kṛṣṇa's higher nature (*param bhāvam*), disdain Him as He engages in a humanlike form [9.11].

Kṛṣṇa describes this *higher nature*, which the foolish and irrational cannot understand. Thus when Arjuna asks Kṛṣṇa to explain *brahman*, spirit [8.1], Kṛṣṇa replies that *brahman* is the supreme unperishing being, and that its nature is Higher Self [8.3]. Here it is important to note that the Sanskrit word used for *nature* is *bhāva*. Kṛṣṇa specifically says that Higher Self is *brahman*'s "own, or personal, nature" (*sva-bhāva*).

Kṛṣṇa also says that beyond even the most subtle region of this world (the *avyakta*) is another, eternal nature. Here too the word for *nature* is *bhāva*. Thus there is no doubt that Kṛṣṇa's *param bhāva* (higher nature or state of being) is eternal, *brahman* or spiritual existence. Yet He is personal, as explained elaborately in this work.

When Kṛṣṇa speaks of His *form* in 9.11, He uses the word *tanu*. This word was not included earlier in the list of *Gītā* words used to mean "body" because *tanu* also means *person* or *self*.[8] The word *tanu* is thus found at 7.21, where Kṛṣṇa states that He bestows unmoving faith to whoever wishes to worship whatever *tanu*. In this context, *tanu* clearly refers to the form, personality or self not of God, but of a particular *god*.

Thus when Kṛṣṇa speaks of the foolish deriding Him when He appears to us as a humanlike *tanu*, we cannot automatically conclude that Kṛṣṇa is describing His own body as a material form that covers His real Self. After all, Kṛṣṇa's body is inconceivable [8.9]. This general point was covered in my discussion of God's body.

---

[8] "*Tanu* also means *person*, or *self*," as in the expressions *svakā tanu*, "one's own person" or *iyaṁ tanur mama*, "this is my self." These examples are from Monier-Williams.

PART XIII
Conclusion

I began this essay by noting that the ancient *Bhagavad-gītā* is a small book that has packed a huge spiritual punch for millennia. Encased in the epic *Mahā-bhārata*, and spoken by the Godhead Kṛṣṇa Himself, the *Gītā* lifts us, systematically and rationally, from the depths of existential despair to the glowing heights of eternal bliss.

The journey begins with a simple distinction that Kṛṣṇa drills home to his suffering, bewildered friend Arjuna: you and I have always existed and always will exist. God has created an ephemeral material world, including our earth, where souls who are so inclined may try as long as they like to exploit matter. We do so by entering mortal bodies, identifying with those bodies as if we were matter, and then trying our best to possess what we like and avoid what we dislike among nature's fleeting offerings.

Trapped in this mundane duality, we entirely forget our eternal identity. Like a vain man who exults when dressed well, and grieves when dressed poorly, we grasp our bodily covering as our self and thus bank our fortunes on the fickle tides of bodily success and pleasure.

And so we wander the universe, under the laws of *karma*, taking on high and low bodies according to the virtue or malice of our acts, and suffering repeated birth, old age, disease and death.

Trapped in the agony and excitement of this cosmic costume party, we forget that we are all wearing material masks, and that our real identity is immeasurably greater than all the mortal roles we so proudly play.

To awaken and redeem us, Lord Kṛṣṇa personally comes to this world and teaches us. That teaching is *Bhagavad-gītā*. Lord Kṛṣṇa urges us not to cling to matter, to detach ourselves so that we are free to ascend to our true spiritual life. To do this, we must see that all material experiences, be they pleasing or displeasing, are mere products of three primary *qualities* or *modes* of life: (mundane) virtue, passion and darkness. All souls, and the God who loves them, exist beyond these modal coverings.

Respecting our individual natures, Kṛṣṇa offers us a variety of disciplined methods, *yoga* paths, all leading to our liberation and enlightenment. "Ordinary" people who go to work, maintain families and live *in the world* may achieve perfection through *karma-yoga*. Those inclined to a more retired life of study and philosophy may attain liberation through *jñāna-yoga*. For the mystics, the *Gītā*'s divine menu offers *dhyāna-yoga*, the path of meditation. Yet Kṛṣṇa emphasizes that the highest path is to devote oneself fully to Him in *bhakti-yoga*, the *yoga* of pure love.

An essential common dynamic runs through all these paths: they must all be performed as a spiritual offering, *yajña*, to the Supreme. Kṛṣṇa emphasizes that we are entitled to do the duty born of our nature, but we cannot claim the fruit of our work. That belongs to God. We receive life itself, our power to reason, and our will to be productive as gifts of the Lord. Thus by offering back the fruits of our God-enabled work, we keep a cosmic wheel turning, the cycle of reciprocity, of receiving and giving back, which forms the basis of justice, civilization and love itself. Thus to embrace any of the *yoga* paths is to offer one's nature to its Source, making our lives, and the universe, whole.

Ultimately, we are divine parts of God, but now selfish desires cover our divine awareness. The *Gītā* shows us how we can easily uncover—literally discover—our pure awareness. Just as pure water is naturally clear and cleansing, so pure consciousness is, by nature, transparent and blissful.

When the world as a global community again turns the cosmic wheel, offering back the fruits of our political, economic, cultural, social and intellectual pursuits to the Source of all, earth itself will regain its original divine nature and people will be happy.

In pure consciousness, one can finally see Kṛṣṇa Himself in His amazing spiritual form, which is materially inconceivable. Arjuna attained this highest goal by his full devotion to God. And Arjuna, after all, is the ideal student of the *Bhagavad-gītā*.

I have tried my best to take you deep into the *Gītā*'s original Sanskrit text, and to share with you the wonders to be seen there. May the *Gītā* be your lifelong friend as you advance toward your personal perfection.[1]

Completed on December 28, 2013
Santa Monica, California

[1] Knowing that few readers of *Bhagavad-gītā* are fluent in Sanskrit, I have endeavored throughout this work to help the reader penetrate the original text, occasionally translating or paraphrasing the same verse in various ways so as to indicate its semantic range.

Literal Translation of *Bhagavad-gītā*

Chapter 1

Dhṛta-rāṣṭra said: On the *dharma*-field,[1] the Kuru-field, my
sons and Pāṇḍu's sons assembled, eager to fight. What did they
do, Sañjaya? 1

Sañjaya said: Seeing the Pāṇḍava[2] army deployed, King
Duryodhana approached his teacher and spoke these words: 2

O Teacher, behold Pāṇḍu's sons' great army, deployed by
your astute student, Drupada's son. 3 Here are heroes, great
archers equal in battle to Bhīma and Arjuna: Yuyudhāna,
Virāṭa and *Great Chariot*[3] Drupada; 4 Dhṛṣṭaketu, Cekitāna,
Kuntibhoja, Purujit; Śaibya, leader of men, and the heroic Kāśi
king;[4] 5 bold Yudhāmanyu, valiant Uttamaujas, Subhadrā's son
and Drupada's sons—all of them *Great Chariots*. 6

O Best of Twice-born,[5] know too the excellent men
that lead my army. I mention them for mutual understanding: 7 you, sir, and so too Bhīṣma, Karṇa, battle-winning Kṛpa,
Aśvatthāmā and Saumadatti. 8 Many other heroes are ready
to give their lives for me; all expert in battle, they strike with

---

[1] Dharma signifies justice, sacred law, duty. Dharma is also a divine cosmic force that rewards those who respect it and punishes those who violate it. Thus the *Bhagavad-gītā* begins on a sacred field that favors justice.

[2] Pāṇḍavas are the sons of Pāṇḍu.

[3] *Great Chariot* is a common epithet of a great chariot fighter.

[4] A note to Sanskrit scholars: for purposes of readability, clarity and/or rhythm of language, minor alterations in the order of listed names or items will be occasionally found in this translation.

[5] Twice-born denotes those of the three higher classes (teachers, rulers and merchants/farmers) who were culturally "reborn" upon receiving sacred instruction.

diverse weapons. 9 Shielded by Bhīṣma, our force is complete; but their force, guarded by Bhīma, is wanting. 10 Standing firm at all assigned posts, every one of you protect Bhīṣma! 11

Rousing his[6] spirits, the senior Kuru, the grandfather,[7] blew his conch loudly, trumpeting forth a lion's sound. 12 Next war drums, kettledrums, cymbals, conches and horns were suddenly struck and blown; the sound grew tumultuous. 13

Then Mādhava and Pāṇḍava,[8] standing on a great swift chariot yoked with white horses, blew their divine conches. 14 Hṛṣīkeśa[9] blew Pāñcajanya, Dhanañjaya blew Devadatta. Vṛkodara[10] of terrific deeds blew the great conch Pauṇḍra. 15 King Yudhiṣṭhira, Kuntī's son, blew Anantavijaya. Nakula and Sahadeva blew Sughoṣa and Maṇipuṣpaka. 16 Virāṭa, Dhṛṣṭadyumna, Great archer Kāśya, *Great Chariot* Śikhaṇḍī, unconquered Sātyaki, 17 Subhadrā's great-armed son, and also Drupada and sons, all blew conches in turn, O lord of wide earth. 18 That great sound, shaking sky and land, rent the hearts of Dhṛta-rāṣṭra's sons. 19

On seeing Dhṛta-rāṣṭra's sons arrayed for battle, O lord of wide earth, Pāṇḍava Arjuna[11], lifting his bow, about to fire missiles, spoke these words to Hṛṣīkeśa [Kṛṣṇa]. 20

Arjuna said: O Acyuta,[12] place my car between both armies as I observe those standing firm, eager to fight. 21 With whom must I contend in this great war effort? 22 I behold those

---

[6] Duryodhana's

[7] Bhīṣma

[8] Mādhava and Pāṇḍava indicates Kṛṣṇa and Arjuna.

[9] Hṛṣīkeśa: Kṛṣṇa; Dhanañjaya indicates Arjuna; Wolf-belly indicates Bhīma, Arjuna's older brother.

[10] Vṛkodara: Bhīma, "Wolf-belly," a voracious eater.

[11] Arjuna, carrying the great monkey Hanuman on his war banner, is here called Kapi-dhvaja, *Monkey-banner.*

[12] Acyuta: the Infallible, Kṛṣṇa

gathered here ready to fight, eager to please Dhṛta-rāṣṭra's evil-
minded son in battle. 23

Sañjaya said: O Bhārata,[13] thus addressed by Guḍākeśa
[Arjuna], Hṛṣīkeśa placed that supreme chariot between both
armies. 24 In front of Bhīṣma, Droṇa and all wide earth's rulers,
He said, "Arjuna, behold these assembled Kurus." 25

There Arjuna beheld grandfathers, teachers, uncles,
brothers, sons, grandsons and friends, fathers-in-law and
well-wishers, standing in both armies. 26 Gazing at all his
kin standing firm, Arjuna despaired; filled with great pity, he
spoke this. 27

Arjuna said: O Kṛṣṇa, seeing our own people standing
near, eager to fight, my limbs weaken and my mouth dries
up. 28 My body trembles, my hairs stand up, Gāṇḍīva[14] slips
from my hand and, truly, my skin burns. 29 I have no power
to stand, my mind reels, O Kṛṣṇa, and I see ill omens. 30 I
foresee no good, Kṛṣṇa, in killing our own people in battle, and
seek neither victory nor kingdom nor pleasures. 31 What is a
kingdom to us, Kṛṣṇa? What are worldly pleasures, or life itself,
when those for whose sake we seek kingdom, pleasures and
joys—32 those very persons—confront us in battle, sacrific-
ing life and fortune: teachers, fathers, sons and grandfathers; 33
uncles, fathers-in-law, grandsons, brothers-in-law and other
close kin? I do not want to kill them even if they are killing us,
Madhusūdana—34 not for a cosmic kingdom, far less for Great
Earth. O Kṛṣṇa, Janārdana, what joy can there be in slaying
Dhṛta-rāṣṭra's sons? 35

Sin would rest on us if we kill these aggressors; thus we
should not kill Dhṛta-rāṣṭra's sons and other kinsmen. How
indeed can we be happy killing our own people, Kṛṣṇa? 36
Even if they, with greed-infected minds, do not see the crime

---

[13] Bhārata: Dhṛta-rāṣṭra.

[14] Gāṇḍīva: Arjuna's famous bow.

in ruining a family or the offense in harming friends, 37 we do clearly see the evil caused by ruining a family, O Janardana. How can we not know this? How then can we not renounce this sin? 38

When family is ruined, everlasting family *dharmas* are lost; when *dharma* is lost, *a-dharma*[15] conquers the entire family. 39 When *a-dharma* conquers, family women are defiled; when women are defiled, Kṛṣṇa, class confusion[16] arises. 40 Such confusion leads only to hell for family killers and family. Forefathers fall, deprived of rice and water rites. 41 These crimes of family killers produce class confusion, destroying lineage-*dharmas* and everlasting family-*dharmas*. 42 Human beings with devastated family *dharmas* surely dwell in hell, Janārdana. Thus we have heard. 43 Oh alas! Greedy for royal happiness, we resolve to do great evil, ready to kill our own people. 44 If Dhṛta-rāṣṭra's sons, weapons in hand, were to kill me, weaponless and unresisting in battle, that would be better for me. 45

Sañjaya said: Thus speaking on the battlefield, giving up bow and arrows, Arjuna sat down on the chariot, his mind torn with grief. 46

---

[15] *a-dharma*: dharma's opposite: injustice, law breaking and dereliction of duty.

[16] *Class-confusion*: *varṇa-saṅkara*

Chapter 2

Sañjaya said: When pity thus possessed Arjuna and tears filled his confused eyes, Madhusūdana[1] spoke these words. 1

The Lord said: In this challenge, how does weakness come upon you? The noble do not welcome it, Arjuna, for it leads not to heaven but to infamy. 2 Do not cede to impotence, Pārtha; it does not become you, Scorcher of Foes. Forgo petty weakness of heart and stand up! 3

Arjuna said: Bhīṣma and Droṇa deserve my honor, Madhusūdana. How can I counterattack them with arrows in battle, O Enemy-slayer? 4 Better to even live by begging in this world than to kill such mentors. For I would live from blood-tinged spoils by killing such greatly noble mentors, though they covet profit. 5 Nor do we know which is worthier for us: that we conquer them or they conquer us. Dhṛta-rāṣṭra's sons stand before us. Killing them, we shall not wish to live. 6

Mistaken pity has weakened my nature. Baffled about duty, I ask You, what would be the certain good? Tell me, I am your disciple; teach me, for I am surrendered to you. 7 I do not see what could dispel the grief drying my senses—even winning an unrivaled thriving kingdom on earth, with the sovereignty of gods. 8

Sañjaya said: Thus addressing Hṛṣīkeśa, foe-burning Guḍākeśaḥ[2] told Govinda,[3] "I shall not fight," and fell silent. 9

---

[1] Kṛṣṇa Who killed the demon Madhu.

[2] Hṛṣīkeśaṁ: Kṛṣṇa, Lord of the senses; Guḍākeśaḥ indicates Arjuna, who conquers sleep, or who has thick hair.

[3] Govinda: Kṛṣṇa.

O Bhārata, in the midst of two armies, Hṛṣīkeśa, almost laughing, spoke these words to despairing Arjuna. 10

The Lord said: You lament what is not lamentable and yet utter wise words. The learned lament neither the departed nor those not departed. 11 Never did I not exist, nor you, nor these rulers of people; nor indeed shall we ever not be. 12 As in the body, the embodied soul experiences childhood, youth and old age, so too one attains another body. This does not confuse the wise. 13

Kaunteya, material contacts like heat and cold give pleasure and pain; impermanent, they come and go. Tolerate them, Bhārata. 14 O Best of Men, a wise person, equal in pain and pleasure, undisturbed by these contacts, earns immortality. 15

The unreal has no existence, the real no nonexistence. In fact, truth-seers have seen the certainty of both. 16 Know the indestructible that pervades all this; no one can destroy that which does not perish. 17 These bodies of the eternal, indestructible, immeasurable embodied soul are said to end. Therefore, Bhārata, fight! 18 Neither one who thinks the soul a killer nor one who thinks it killed understands. The soul neither kills nor is killed. 19 The soul is never born and never dies, nor having existed will it ever not be. Unborn, eternal, everlasting, primeval, it is not killed when the body is killed. 20

Pārtha, knowing the soul to be indestructible, eternal, unborn and unperishing, how does one kill and whom does one kill or cause to kill? 21 As one dons new clothes, discarding those that are worn, so the embodied soul, discarding worn bodies, dons new ones. 22

Weapons do not cut the soul; fire does not burn it; water does not wet it; wind does not wither it. 23 The soul cannot be cut, burned, wetted or withered. It is eternal, goes everywhere, yet it is stationary, immovable and everlasting. 24 The soul is said to be unmanifest, inconceivable and immutable. Knowing it thus, you should not lament. 25

And even if you believe the soul is always born and always dies, Great-armed, you should not lament it. 26 Indeed, for one born, death is fixed, as birth is fixed for the dead. Therefore, in an unavoidable matter you should not lament. 27 Beings are unmanifest at first, manifest at midpoint and surely unmanifest at the end, Bhārata. What do you lament in this, Arjuna? 28

Someone sees the soul as a wonder, another speaks of it as a wonder, and still another hears of it as a wonder. Yet some, even after hearing, do not comprehend it. 29 The embodied soul in each and every body never can be killed; thus you ought not grieve for any being. 30

And also, considering your *dharma*, you should not falter. For a warrior there is nothing better than righteous battle. 31 Happy, Pārtha, are warriors who gain such battle that comes of its own, opening wide heaven's gate. 32 Now if you will not fight this righteous battle then, giving up your *dharma* and reputation, you will incur sin. 33 People will proclaim your perpetual infamy; and for the highly esteemed, infamy is worse than death. 34 *Great Chariots*[4] will think you fled the fight in fear; you will be shamed before those who gave you high regard. 35 Your enemies will ridicule your power, speaking many unutterable things. What pain is worse than this? 36 If slain, you will reach heaven; conquering, you will rule Great Earth. Therefore, arise Kaunteya! Decide for battle! 37 Treating as equal pleasure and pain, gain and loss, victory and defeat, engage for war and incur no sin. 38

This is reason, analytically taught. Now hear of it in practice. With such reason, Pārtha, you will cast off *karma*'s bonds. 39 Effort does not fail here; there is no falling back. Even very little of this *dharma* delivers one from great danger. 40 Herein, Kuru-son, determined reason is one, whereas the reasoning of the undetermined is many-branched, indeed endless. 41

---

[4] Great chariot fighters.

Intent on heaven, unwise selfish souls delight in Veda-speech, Pārtha. Claiming there is *nothing else*, they proclaim those florid words that abound in rituals, afford good birth and fruits of action, and lead to assets and power. 42–43 For those that cling to assets and power, their minds carried off by these, full-focused determined reason does not take place. 44 The Vedas center on three qualities;[5] go beyond the three qualities, Arjuna—beyond duality. Stand always in goodness, self-possessed, with no care to acquire. 45 To a knowing *brāhmaṇa*, all the Vedas have as much value as a well when, all about, wide waters stream. 46

You have a right to action alone, never to its fruits. Neither be motivated by action's fruits nor cling to inaction. 47 Firm in *yoga*, perform deeds without attachment, being equal in success and failure; for *yoga* is said to be equality, Dhanañjaya. 48

Action is by far inferior to the practice of reason, Dhanañjaya; seek shelter in reason. Miserly are those motivated by fruits. 49 Joined to reason, one forsakes both good and bad action in this life. As such, prepare for *yoga*! *Yoga* is mastery in actions. 50 Joined to reason, the mindful forsake action-born fruits. Saved from birth bondage, they go to the place free of malady. 51

When your reason will cross over the illusion-thicket, then you will be indifferent to what was heard and is to be heard. 52 When your hearing-confounded[6] reason stands unwavering, unmoving, in full concentration—then you will attain *yoga*. 53

---

[5] The three qualities are goodness, passion and darkness—the three qualities of all material things and experiences.

[6] Hearing is *śruti*, in Sanskrit, indicating the *karma-kāṇḍa* portion dealing with mundane rituals aiming at material gain. The previous verse, 2.52, also refers to this with the words "*all that was heard and is to be heard*" (*śrotavyasya śrutasya ca*). See also verses 2.42–45, which also urge indifference to the mundane portions of the Vedas.

Arjuna said: Keśava, what is the language of one firm in wisdom, fixed in full concentration? What does the steady-minded say, and why stay or go? 54

The Lord said: When one, satisfied by self in self alone, rejects all the mind's selfish desires, Pārtha, one is said to have firm wisdom. 55 Free of passion, fear and anger, with mind undisturbed in miseries, one no longer longing for pleasures is said to be a steady-minded sage. 56 Wisdom is firmly fixed in one who is everywhere unaffected whether meeting good or evil—who neither delights nor despises. 57 Wisdom is firmly fixed in one who fully withdraws the senses from their objects as the tortoise withdraws its limbs. 58

Sense objects recede for the embodied soul who abstains from them, but taste remains; yet even taste ceases on seeing something better. 59 Kaunteya, even though an inspired person endeavors, turbulent senses take the mind by force. 60 Controlling all these senses, one must stay linked, devoted to Me. Wisdom is firmly fixed in one who rules the senses. 61

When a person contemplates sense objects, attachment for them arises. Desire springs from attachment, and from desire, anger is born. 62 From anger comes confusion; from confusion, memory loss; from memory loss, reason's ruin. By reason's ruin, self vanishes. 63

Engaging sense objects with self-controlled senses, free of delight and hate, the accomplished soul attains clarity. 64 In clarity, the letting go of all sorrows ensues. With a clear mind, reason quickly grows steady. 65

The unlinked does not reason. The unlinked does not focus. The unfocused has no peace. And for one not at peace, where is happiness? 66 In fact, as senses roam, that sense to which mind yields takes away one's wisdom as wind takes away a boat at sea. 67 Therefore, Great-armed, wisdom is firmly fixed in one who fully restrains senses from sense objects. 68

In the night of all beings, the self-controlled awakes, and beings awake in the seeing sage's night. 69 As the sea stands steady, unmoving as waters enter and fill it, so one in whom all desires thus enter attains peace, not one who desires [to enjoy] desires. 70 Giving up all desires, a person who lives free of longing, free of *I* and *mine*, achieves peace. 71 This is the Brahman status, Arjuna, achieving which one is not confused, standing in which, even at end time, one rises to *nirvāṇa*[7] in Brahman. 72

---

[7] *Nirvāṇa* means "cessation, extinction"—in this case, of all the material passions that cause suffering and rebirth. *Nirvāṇa* in Brahman, the Absolute, indicates that one's material desires cease upon achieving a higher spiritual object—as taught in Bg 2.59.

Chapter 3

Arjuna said: Keṣava, if you think reason better than action, then why do you engage me in horrible action? 1 By this equivocal instruction, you simply confuse my reason. To resolve this, speak that one thing by which I can achieve the greater good. 2

The Lord said: I already told you, sinless one, that the steady way is two-fold in this world: for the analytic, it is by knowledge-*yoga*, and for the active, by action-*yoga*. 3 One does not enjoy freedom from action by not undertaking actions, nor does one fully attain perfection by renunciation alone. 4 In fact, no one ever remains inactive, not even for a moment; nature's modes force everyone to act. 5 One who restrains action senses,[1] yet goes on thinking of sense objects in the mind, is a confused soul whose conduct is said to be false. 6 Better, Arjuna, is one who takes up action-*yoga* with action senses, mentally restraining the senses. 7 Perform required action, for action is better than inaction; you cannot even achieve bodily maintenance without action. 8

This world is *karma*[2] bondage, except for *karma* (action) done for offering. Perform action for that purpose, Arjuna, free of attachment. 9 Of old, the lord of creatures sent forth creatures *with sacrifice* and said:

"By *this* shall you flourish! Let *this* yield your chosen desires. 10 Prosper the gods by *this*, and let the gods prosper you. Prospering one another, you will achieve the highest good. 11

---

[1] The five *action senses* are hands, legs, voice, reproductive organ and excretion organ.

[2] The Sanskrit word *karma* literally means *action*. Every action not done for sacrifice produces a reaction, binding us to this world.

Prospered by sacrifice, the gods will certainly give you desired enjoyments. One who enjoys these gifts without giving back to the givers is merely a thief. 12 Eating sacrifice remnants, the virtuous are freed of all offense. But the wretched that cook for themselves eat sin. 13 Beings live from food. Food arises from rain. Rain comes from sacrifice. Sacrifice arises from duty. 14 Know that duty comes forth from *brahman*. *Brahman* springs from the Imperishable. Therefore, all-pervading *brahman* ever abides in sacrifice." 15

A cycle is thus made to turn. One who does not keep it turning, a sense enjoyer of errant life, lives in vain, Pārtha. 16 But a human being who can delight in self alone, self-content, satisfied in self alone, has no duty. 17 That person has no interest in acting or not acting, nor in depending on any being. 18 Therefore, ever detached, perform action. A detached person thus performing action surely reaches transcendence. 19 Indeed, by action alone, kings like Janaka rose to perfection. Simply considering the world's welfare, you should act. 20

Whatever the greatest one does, common people do just the same, following the standard he sets. 21 Pārtha, in the three worlds there is nothing I *must* do, nothing that I have not achieved or *must* achieve. Yet still I engage in action. 22 Truly Pārtha, if ever I ceased to carefully engage in action, people would all follow my path. 23 These worlds would fall to ruin if I did not perform action. I would cause confusion. I would harm these creatures. 24

Bhārata, just as the unwise act attached to action, so the wise should act unattached, seeking the world's welfare. 25 The wise, linked in *yoga*, should not produce a rupture in the reason[3] of the ignorant attached to action, but rather should encourage all duties by performing them. 26

---

[3] Rupture in the reason: Ordinary people are attached to their worldly duties. If a sage preaches renunciation to them, they may lose enthusiasm for their worldly duties and still be unable to live a pure spiritual life. It is better,

Actions are being done entirely by nature's modes; a soul bewildered by egotism believes "I am the doer." 27 But knowing true principles, O Great-armed, realizing that *modes are functioning in modes*, one clings to neither mode nor action. 28 Those confused by nature's modes cling to mode actions.[4] One who knows all should not deviate the unwitting, who do not know all. 29

Relinquishing all actions to Me by awareness of higher self, becoming free from hankering and possessiveness, fight without fever. 30 Those persons that ever abide by this My conclusion, trusting and not envying, are surely freed of *karma*. 31 But those that resent and do not abide by My conclusion—know them to be lost and mindless, confused about all knowledge. 32

Even one with knowledge acts according to one's nature. Beings follow their nature. What will repression do? 33 Attachment and aversion abide in each sense object. One should not come under their control, for they surely obstruct one's path. 34 Better is one's own imperfect *dharma* than another's *dharma* well performed. Loss in one's own *dharma* is better, for another's *dharma* carries danger. 35

Arjuna said: So what impels a person to commit sin, even unwilling, as if engaged by force? 36

The Lord said: It is lust, it is rage, springing from the passion mode. This is the great devourer, the great evil. Know it here as the enemy. 37 It covers this world as smoke covers fire, dust covers a mirror, the womb covers an embryo. 38 Kaunteya, this perennial foe in the form of lust, this unquenchable fire,

---

Kṛṣṇa teaches, to encourage such people to perform their duties and offer the fruits of their work to Him. Thus *karma*, worldly work, becomes *karma-yoga*, a spiritual practice that allows people to continue in their family and vocational duties.

[4] Mode actions: actions performed within the three mundane modes (*guṇas*): goodness, passion and darkness (*sattva*, *rajas*, *tamas*). Spiritual acts are *guṇa-atīta*, beyond the mundane modes. See verses 14.21, 25, 26.

covers the knower's knowledge. 39 It is said to dwell in senses, mind and reason, and through them, bewilders the embodied soul, covering knowledge. 40 Therefore, Best of Bharatas, first controlling the senses, slay this evil that destroys knowledge and wisdom. 41

They say that senses are superior, and beyond senses is mind. Reason is yet beyond mind. But this [soul] is beyond reason. 42 Thus reasoning to what is beyond reason,[5] steadying self by self, O Great-armed, slay this treacherous foe in the form of lust. 43

[5] Reasoning to what is beyond reason: reason should grasp its own limits and pursue the highest knowledge through devotion. Though reason alone cannot reach to God, God's revelation, rightly understood, is reasonable.

Chapter 4

The Lord said: I taught this imperishable *Yoga* to Vivasvān;
Vivasvān told Manu; Manu spoke to Ikṣvāku. 1 King-sages
thus learned it as received in [disciplic] succession. After great
time here, it was lost. 2 Today I teach you this same ancient
Yoga, indeed this supreme mystery, for you are My devotee and
friend. 3

Arjuna said: Your birth is later, Vivasvān's birth earlier.
How is it that at first You taught him? 4

The Lord said: Both you and I have passed through many
births, Arjuna. I know them all, you do not, Scorcher of Foes. 5
Even though I am the unborn, unchanging Soul and Lord of
beings, I appear by My Self-power, standing upon My own
nature. 6 Bhārata, whenever *dharma* weakens and *a-dharma*
surges, I then manifest My Self. 7 To deliver the righteous,
destroy the wicked and restore *dharma*, I appear in every age. 8
One who thus knows in truth My divine birth and deeds never
again takes birth upon giving up the body, but comes to Me,
Arjuna. 9

Freed of passion, fear and anger, absorbed in Me, many
found shelter in Me. Purified by austerity and knowledge, they
came to My state of being. 10 However anyone approaches Me,
I accept them in just that way. Human beings wholly follow My
path, Pārtha. 11

Longing for success in actions, people here offer to deities. Success born of action comes quickly in the human
realm. 12 According to divisions of mode and action, I created

the four-*varṇa* system.[1] Though I made it, know me as the changeless non-maker.[2] 13 Actions do not taint Me, nor do I covet action's fruits. One who thus knows Me is not bound by actions. 14 Knowing this, even the ancients, seeking liberation, performed action. Therefore, perform action exactly as did the ancients in ancient times. 15

What is action? What is inaction? Even sages are confused here. Thus I shall explain action to you, knowing which you will be freed from evil. 16 Indeed one must discern action, one must discern wrong action, and one must discern inaction. Deep is action's way. 17 One who can see inaction in action and action in inaction is discerning among human beings, and is linked while performing all actions. 18

The discerning say that one whose every endeavor is devoid of selfish intent is a sage whose *karma* is burned by knowledge-fire. 19 Giving up attachment to action's fruit, ever content and independent—though engaged in action, one actually does nothing at all. 20 Free of longing, with mind and self restrained, abandoning all ownership and performing action only to sustain the body, one incurs no sin. 21

Fully content with spontaneous gain, beyond duality, free of envy, equal in success and failure—even acting, one is not bound. 22 *Karma* is completely dissolved for one free of attachment, who is liberated, acting for sacrifice, with mind fixed in knowledge. 23 The offering is *brahman*: *brahman* pours *brahman*-oblation into *brahman*-fire; and by that full focus on *brahman*-action, *brahman* alone is to be attained. 24

---

[1] "Four-*varṇa* system" indicates the four vocational orders: *brāhmaṇas* (teachers and priests); *kṣatriyas* (rulers and warriors); *vaiśyas* (farmers and merchants); *śūdras* (workers, servants, helpers of all sorts.)

[2] *"Know me as the changeless non-maker"*: Kṛṣṇa performs no selfish activities, and as a pure spiritual being, He has no duty within the four-*varṇa* system He creates. Thus He is the non-maker, or non-doer.

Some *yogīs* worshipfully sacrifice to gods alone. Some, by sacrifice alone, offer sacrifice into *brahman*-fire. 25 Others offer senses such as hearing into the self-control fire. Others offer sense objects such as sound into the sense-fire. 26 Some offer all sense actions or breath actions into the *yoga* fire of self-control, ignited by knowledge. 27 So too, some strivers of strict vows [enact] object-sacrifice,[3] austerity-sacrifice, *yoga*-sacrifice or knowledge-sacrifice by sacred study. 28 Some offer in-breath to out-breath or out-breath to in-breath. Stopping in-out-breath movements, they rely on breath control. Some restrain eating and offer in-breaths to in-breaths. 29 All these do indeed know sacrifice; sacrifice removes their sins. Eating the nectar-remnant of sacrifice, they go to eternal Brahman. 30 O Best of Kurus, one who does not sacrifice has not this world. How then the next? 31

Thus manifold sacrifices have spread facing Brahman. Know them all to be action-born; knowing thus, you will be liberated. 32 Pārtha, Scorcher of Foes, better than object-sacrifice is knowledge-sacrifice, for each and every action culminates in knowledge. 33

Learn this by submission, full inquiry and service. Knowers will teach you knowledge for they have seen the Truth. 34 Thus knowing, you will not return to illusion, Pāṇḍava, for you will thus see all beings in the Self—that is, in Me. 35

Even if you are most sinful among all sinners, by the knowledge-boat alone you will cross over all evil. 36 Arjuna, as blazing fire turns kindling to ashes, so knowledge-fire turns all *karma* to ashes. 37 In this world, there is no purifier like knowledge. In time, one perfected in *yoga* personally finds it in self. 38 A faithful person gains knowledge and is devoted to it, with senses fully controlled. Gaining knowledge, one soon achieves

---

[3] Object-sacrifice: offering material objects such as butter into fire or offering typical worship articles such as incense, lamp, water, cloth, flower and fan or offering some of one's assets to a deity.

supreme peace. 39 The unknowing, unbelieving, doubting soul comes to nothing. Neither this world, nor one higher, nor joy belong to the doubting soul. 40

Dhanañjaya, actions do not bind one who has renounced action through *yoga*, slashed doubt by knowledge and regained self. 41 Your heart's doubt is born of ignorance. Therefore, severing it with the knowledge-sword, stand on *yoga*! Stand up Bhārata! 42

Chapter 5

Arjuna said: Kṛṣṇa, You praise renunciation of actions and then
again *yoga*.[1] Tell me definitely, which of the two is better. 1

The Lord said: Both renunciation [of actions] and action-
yoga confer the highest good. But of the two, action-*yoga* is
superior to renouncing action. 2 One who neither hates nor
hankers is to be known as a constant renouncer beyond duality,
easily freed from bondage, O Great-armed. 3

The childish, not the wise, claim that analysis and practice
are distinct. A person who properly performs but one attains
the fruit of both. 4 The status achieved by analytic methods is
also attained by *yoga* practices. One who sees that analysis and
practice are one [truly] sees. 5

Yet renunciation is difficult to achieve without *yoga*,
O Great-armed. Linked in *yoga*, a sage soon achieves the
Absolute. 6 Linked in *yoga*, a purified self who conquers self
and senses—a self, being the self of all beings[2]—is not tainted
though acting. 7

"I do nothing at all." Thus a linked truth-knower should
think. While seeing, hearing, touching, smelling, eating, going,
dreaming, 8 breathing, chatting, letting go, grasping, even opening and closing the eyes—one should hold this conviction: *the
senses move in sense objects*. 9 Giving up attachment, entrusting
actions to the Absolute, one is not tainted by sin—like a lotus
leaf untouched by water. 10 With body, mind, reason and even

[1] Arjuna takes *yoga* to be spiritual action, incompatible with giving up action.

[2] "Being the self of all beings" indicates the attainment of full spiritual empathy.

pure senses, *yogīs* perform action for self-purification, giving up attachment. 11

Linked in *yoga*, giving up action's fruit, one achieves enduring peace. Unlinked, clinging to the fruit, one is bound by selfish action. 12 Mentally renouncing all actions, a self-ruling embodied soul stays happily in the Nine-gated City,[3] neither acting nor causing to act. 13

The Lord creates neither agency nor actions for persons, nor their tie to action's fruit; one's own nature prevails. 14 The Almighty does not assume anyone's sin or good deed. Ignorance covers knowledge; it bewilders people. 15 But for those whose ignorance of self is destroyed by knowledge, sun-like knowledge reveals the Supreme. 16 Those whose reason, self, devotion and refuge rest in Him—they go to *non-return*, their impurity shaken off by knowledge. 17

The wise see as equal a learned humble *brāhmaṇa*, a cow, an elephant, and even a dog and dog cooker. 18 In this very world, those whose minds stand in equality conquer creation. Brahman is truly equal and flawless. Therefore they stand in Brahman. 19

One should neither rejoice on obtaining that which pleases nor lament on obtaining the displeasing. With steady reason, unconfused, a Brahman-knower stands in Brahman. 20 Detached from external contacts, self finds pleasure in self. Linked by *yoga* to Brahman, that self finds unperishing joy. 21 Indeed those pleasures born of sense-contact are merely sources of pain, Kaunteya, for they begin and end. A sage does not delight in them. 22

Before giving up the body, one who is able to tolerate in this very life the urge born of lust and anger is a happy person, linked in *yoga*. 23 With inner joy, inner delight and real

---

[3] Nine-gated City: the human body with nine gates—two eyes, two ears, two nostrils, mouth, genital and anus.

inner light, such a *yogī*, being Brahman, achieves *nirvāṇa* in Brahman. 24 Self-restrained sages, their sins spent, gain *nirvāṇa* in Brahman. Their duality severed, they delight in the good of every being. 25 For those wise souls freed from desire and anger, who strive with controlled minds, *nirvāṇa* in Brahman comes their way. 26 Putting outside contacts outside, fixing the eyes right between the brows, equalizing in and out breaths moving in the nose, 27 intent on freedom, with senses, mind and reason controlled, with desire, fear and anger gone—ever so, a sage is surely liberated. 28

Knowing Me as the Enjoyer of sacrifice and austerity, the Great Lord of all worlds, and a Kind Friend to all, one attains peace. 29

Chapter 6

The Lord said: Unattached to action's fruit, one who performs
action as duty is the renouncer and the *yogī*, not the fireless[1]
or inactive. 1 What they call *renunciation*, know to be *yoga*,
Pāṇḍava, for no one becomes a *yogī* without renouncing selfish
will. 2 For a sage seeking to rise to *yoga*, action is said to be
the means; only for one raised to *yoga* is ceasing said to be the
means. 3 Surely when one clings to neither sense objects nor
actions, giving up all selfish will, one is then said to have risen
to *yoga*. 4

One should uplift self by self; one should not degrade self.
Indeed self alone is self's friend; self alone is self's foe. 5 Self
is friend to that self by whom self alone is conquered; but that
very self can work as enemy, due to non-self's enmity.[2] 6 For
the peaceful who conquer self, Higher Self[3] is fully established
in cold and heat, joy and sorrow, and so too in honor and dishonor. 7

A soul content with knowledge and wisdom, who stands at
the peak with senses conquered, is said to be linked—a *yogī* for

---

[1] Fireless: one who rejects fire sacrifice or sacrifice in general, symbolized by fire. See 4.25–27 wherein Kṛṣṇa uses the term *agni*, fire, symbolically.

[2] The dense English closely reflects the Sanskrit. The *Gītā* here gives a quite existential doctrine: we must take responsibility for our selves. The self alone is friend or enemy of oneself. The "enmity of non-self" refers to our false ego, our "material bodily self," an illusory identity that works against the eternal soul's ultimate interest.

[3] Higher Self: the Lord dwelling in everyone's heart; having conquered the mind, one reaches the Lord in the heart.

whom clay, stone and gold are equal. 8 Still better is one with equal reason among the kind-hearted, friends, foes, abstainers, mediators, the odious and kindred, and even among saints and sinners. 9

Alone, secluded, self and mind restrained, not covetous or possessive, a *yogī* must always link self in *yoga*. 10 In a pure place, setting not too high or low one's firm seat, layered with cloth, antelope skin and *kuśa* grass 11 —sitting there, making mind single-pointed, thoughts and sense activities restrained, one should practice *yoga* for self-purification. 12 Steady and unmoving, keeping body, head and neck aligned, focusing on the very tip of one's nose, not staring in any direction, 13 self calm, fear gone, chastity vow firm, thoughts in Me, controlling the mind—one should stay linked in *yoga*, dedicated to Me. 14 Thus constantly linking self, a *yogī* of disciplined mind attains *nirvāṇa* of highest peace, which abides in Me. 15

Yet *yoga* does not happen for one who overeats or solely fasts, nor for one who habitually sleeps too much or simply stays awake. 16 [But] sorrow-ending *yoga*[4] does occur for one in whose actions there is proper[5] eating and recreation, proper effort, proper sleeping and wakefulness. 17 When the strictly controlled mind abides in self alone, not pursuing any selfish wish, then one is said to be linked in *yoga*. 18 A *yogī* of controlled mind, practicing *yoga* of self, is compared to a wind-screened lamp that does not flicker. 19

---

[4]The word *yoga*, from the verbal root *yuj*, means many things, but its root meaning is *to link, connect,* etc. This verse repeatedly employs the cognate *yukta*, usually translated here as *linked* (see the following note). Thus Kṛṣṇa makes a clear point: the *yoga*-link occurs for those who link their activities to the Absolute through devotion, sacrifice, etc., as often explained in the *Gītā*.

[5]Proper is *yukta* in Sanskrit, which also means *linked*. Eating, sleeping, etc. are *proper* when they are linked to the will of God, and thus support a successful spiritual practice aimed at returning to God.

That in which mind grows quiet, held fast by *yoga* practice, in which one is content by seeing self in Self by self,[6] 20 in which one knows endless joy beyond the senses, a joy acceptable to reason, where once standing one does not move from truth, 21 and gaining which, one realizes there is no greater gain, standing in which, one is not deviated even by heavy sorrow—22 that is called *yoga*, the unlinking of the sorrow-link. One is meant to practice *yoga* with conviction and undiscouraged mind. 23

Wholly forsaking all selfish desires born of will and regulating the set of senses by mind alone, 24 one must gradually come to stillness through reason held with resolve. Fixing mind firmly in self, one should reflect on nothing else; 25 and from wherever the unsteady fickle mind wanders one should pull it back, bringing it under control of self alone. 26

Ultimate joy comes to a *yogī* of contented mind and subdued passion, who abstains from impurity, having joined Brahman. 27 Thus a *yogī*, free of impurity and always linking self, joyfully attains endless joy by full contact with Brahman. 28

With equal vision everywhere, the *yoga*-linked self sees Self in all creatures and all creatures in Self. 29 To one who sees Me everywhere and sees everything in Me, I am not lost, nor is that person lost to Me. 30 A *yogī* is one who abides in unity and honors Me in all creatures. However living, that *yogī* lives in Me. 31 By self-comparison, one who sees everywhere equally in joy or sorrow is respected as the highest *yogī*, Arjuna. 32

Arjuna said: This *yoga* with equality that You teach does not seem an enduring state, due to unsteadiness, Madhusūdana. 33 For the mind truly is unsteady, stormy, strong and stubborn, Kṛṣṇa. It seems harder to restrain than the wind. 34

The Lord said: Doubtless, Great-armed, the mind is on the move, hard to hold fast. But one catches it with practice and

---

[6] "*Seeing self in Self by self*": by practicing *yoga*, one sees one's self as part of the Supreme Self within.

dispassion, Kaunteya. 35 I think it hard for an undisciplined soul to achieve *yoga*; but a controlled, striving soul is able to attain it by right means. 36

Arjuna said: Kṛṣṇa, what is the fate of a faithful person whose mind deviates from *yoga*—who stops striving, not achieving *yoga* perfection? 37 Baffled on the spiritual path, both ways lost,[7] with no foundation, does not one perish like a rent cloud? 38 This is my doubt Kṛṣṇa; You ought to fully dispel it. Apart from you, surely there is no other dispeller of this doubt. 39

The Lord said: Pārtha, never in this life or the next is that person ruined. Dear friend, surely no doer of good meets a bad fate. 40 After reaching the worlds of right-doers and dwelling there for myriad years, one fallen from *yoga* takes birth in a pure and prosperous home. 41 Or else one is born in a family of wise *yogīs*. Surely in this world such a birth is much harder to achieve. 42 Therein one reconnects to past life's understanding, and then strives on for perfection, Kuru-child. 43 By that former practice alone, one is inevitably brought back; seeking to know about *yoga*, one surpasses Word-Brahman.[8] 44 Striving with real effort, fully cleansed of impurities, and perfected after several lives, the *yogī* achieves the highest state. 45

A *yogī* surpasses ascetics, and is even held to surpass the learned. A *yogī* surpasses ritualists. Therefore be a *yogī*, Arjuna. 46 And of all *yogīs*, I consider as most linked in *yoga* one whose inner self has gone to Me, who faithfully reveres Me.[9] 47

---

[7] Both ways lost: one jeopardized one's worldly career by spiritual renunciation, then fell from that spiritual practice.

[8] "Word-Brahman" indicates The words of the Veda that teach rites for mundane rewards; see 2.42–46.

[9] Most linked in *yoga*: since the word *yoga* means *link, connection*, etc., to be most linked is to be the most accomplished, successful *linker* or *yogī*.

Chapter 7

The Lord said: Hear, Pārtha, how by practicing *yoga* at My shelter, with mind fixed on Me, you will know Me fully beyond
doubt. 1 I will teach you entirely this knowledge and wisdom,
knowing which, nothing further remains to be known here. 2
Among thousands of persons, one strives for perfection; and of
those who strive and succeed, one knows Me in truth. 3

Earth, water, fire, air, space, mind, reason and egotism—this is My separated eight-fold nature. 4 It is inferior, O
Great-armed, but know of My other superior nature that animates the world: the living being. 5 Understand that these two
natures are the source of all beings—and that I am the origin
and dissolution of the entire cosmos. 6

There is nothing else beyond Me, Dhanañjaya. All this
rests on Me like pearls on thread. 7 I am the taste in water,
Kaunteya, the light of moon and sun, sacred Om in all Vedas,
sound in space, valor in men. 8 I am pure fragrance in earth,
splendor in fire, life in all beings, and austerity in the austere. 9
Know Me, Pārtha, as the perennial seed of all beings, reason
of the rational, splendor of the splendid. 10 Of the strong, I am
strength, free of desire and passion. Among beings, I am desire
that does not oppose *dharma*, O Best of Bharatas. 11 Indeed,
know that all virtuous, passionate and dark states come from
Me alone. Yet I am not in them; they are in Me. 12

Baffled by these three modal states, this whole world does
not recognize Me, Who am above these [states], unchanging. 13
This, My divine modal illusion, is truly difficult to overcome.
Those who approach Me alone, cross beyond this illusion. 14

Those who act badly do not approach Me: the foolish;
the lowest of men; those whose knowledge is robbed by

illusion; those who resort to ungodly states. 15 Four types of beneficent persons worship Me, Arjuna: one who suffers; a knowledge seeker; one who prays for wealth; and one with knowledge, O Best of Bharatas. 16 Of these, the one with knowledge, always linked in singular devotion, is superior. I am exceedingly dear to one with knowledge, and that person is also dear to Me. 17

Truly all these are noble, yet I accept the one with knowledge as My very Self, for that linked soul abides only in Me, the ultimate goal. 18 After many births, one with knowledge approaches Me, knowing, "Vāsudeva [Kṛṣṇa] is everything." That great soul is very hard to find. 19

Following various rules, ruled by their own natures, those robbed of knowledge approach other divinities. 20 Whoever wishes to worship whatever form, faithfully devoted, to each I bestow unmoving faith. 21 With that faith, one undertakes worship and thereby obtains wishes actually bestowed by Me alone. 22 But [only] a fleeting fruit comes to those of little insight. Sacrificers to gods go to gods. My devotees surely go to Me. 23

Not knowing My higher, ultimate, unchanging nature, the unwise think Me a formless existence that takes on visible individuality. 24 I do not reveal Myself to all. This confused world, covered by mystic illusion, does not recognize Me—unborn and unchanging. 25 I know the past, present and future of [all] beings, Arjuna. But no one knows Me. 26

Bhārata, O Scorcher of Foes, due to the bewilderment of duality arising from desire and hate, all beings enter illusion at birth. 27 But those of pious deeds, whose misdeeds have ceased, who are freed from such bewilderment, worship Me with firm vows. 28 Depending on Me, those who strive for release from old age and death understand Brahman *entire*, higher self and action *complete*. 29 With awareness linked in *yoga*, those who know Me as the higher principle of divinity, nature and sacrifice, know me even at the time of passing. 30

Chapter 8

Arjuna said: What is Brahman, what is Higher Self and what
is action, O Ultimate Person? What principle governs nature?
What principle is said to govern the gods? 1 Who governs sacrifice here in this body, Madhusūdana, and how? And how are
disciplined souls to know You at the time of passing? 2

The Lord said: Brahman is the supreme imperishable; its
nature is said to be Higher Self.[1] Creation that generates a being's
state of being is termed *karma*. 3 A perishing state is nature's
principle, and divinity's principle is the Person. I alone, here
in this body, am sacrifice's principle, O Best of Body-bearers. 4

At end-time, one who departs remembering Me alone
while releasing the body, goes to My state of being; of this there
is no doubt. 5 Indeed, one surely attains the very state that
one remembers while quitting the body, Kaunteya, whatever it
may be; for one has always caused that state of being to be.[2] 6
Therefore, at all times remember Me and fight. With reason and
mind focused on Me, you will doubtlessly come to Me alone. 7

With unwavering mind, linked by disciplined *yoga*, one
reaches the supreme divine Person, always thinking of Him. 8
One should remember [Him] as the ancient seer and constant
ruler, smaller than the smallest, the creator of all, with inconceivable form, lustrous like the sun, beyond darkness. 9 At the
time of passing, filled with devotion and yogic power, mind
unmoving, fixing the life air between the eyebrows, one reaches
that supreme divine Person. 10

I shall now briefly describe to you that which knowers of
the Vedas call the unperishing place, into which passion-free

[1] Brahman is ultimately a Supreme Eternal Person.

[2] One bears personal responsibility for one's future states of being.

ascetics enter, desiring which they follow chaste practices. 11 Restraining all [bodily] gates, fixing mind in heart, and placing life air at head's top, one stands on the *yoga* platform. 12 Sounding the Absolute as the single syllable *Om* and steadily remembering Me, one then departs the body and attains the highest destination. 13

Pārtha, I am easy to attain for the ever-linked *yogī* who always remembers Me with ever-unswerving mind. 14 Reaching Me, great souls never return to birth in this transient realm of sorrow, for they have gone to final perfection. 15 All realms, from earth to even Brahmā's abode, are places from which one must return. But on reaching Me, Kaunteya, one is never born again. 16

Those that rightly know day and night, know that Brahmā's day endures for a thousand ages, as does his night. 17 At day's coming, all manifest beings emerge from what is called the unmanifest; and on night's coming, they are reabsorbed right there into the unmanifest. 18 Repeatedly coming into being, Pārtha, this very collection of creatures is helplessly reabsorbed at night and [again] goes forth at day. 19

Still higher than this unmanifest is another eternal unmanifest, which does not perish when all beings are vanishing. 20 They call that imperishable unmanifest the highest path, reaching which they do not return; for that is My supreme abode. 21 By exclusive devotion, one can surely attain that Supreme Person in Whom [all] beings exist and by Whom this whole world is suffused. 22

O Best of Bharatas, I shall now tell you those times at which departing *yogīs* either return or do not return. 23 *Brahman*-knowing persons who depart during fire, light, day, waxing moon and the sun's six-month journey north go to *Brahman*. 24 But that *yogī* returns who departs during smoke, night, waning moon and the sun's six-month journey south, reaching moon's light. 25 Now, these light and dark passages from the world are

considered perpetual; by one path, one does not return, and
by the other, one does. 26 Knowing these two paths, Pārtha, a
yogī is never baffled; be thus always linked in *yoga*, Arjuna. 27
A *yogī*, knowing all this, surpasses whatever auspicious fruit is
indicated in the Vedas, in sacrifices, in penances, and also in
charities—and comes to the supreme, original status. 28

Chapter 9

The Lord said: To you who do not envy, I shall teach this greatest mystery—knowledge joined to wisdom—knowing which you will be freed from misfortune. 1 Sovereign science, sovereign mystery, *this* is the ultimate purifier. Realized by direct perception, it is righteous, very joyful to practice and unperishing. 2 Those that do not trust this *dharma*, do not attain Me, Scorcher of Foes; rather they return to the road of death cycles. 3

I pervade all this world with My invisible feature. All beings stand in Me; I do not stand in them. 4 And [yet] beings do not stand in Me. Behold My ruling *yoga*![1] I sustain beings, and do not stand in them, for My Self causes beings to be. 5 As the great wind going everywhere always stands in space, so realize that all beings stand in Me. 6

At eon's end, Kaunteya, all beings go to My nature; and again, at eon's start, I release them. 7 Utilizing My own nature, again and again I release this entire host of beings, who are powerless in nature's power. 8 And these actions do not bind Me, sitting as one sitting apart, Dhanañjaya—detached from these actions. 9

By My oversight, nature begets the moving and unmoving; by this cause, Kaunteya, the world turns in its cycles. 10 Not knowing My higher state of being as the Great Lord of beings, fools disdain Me as I engage in human form. 11 With vain hopes, vain actions and vain knowledge, the thoughtless cling to a demonic, godless, illusory nature. 12

But great souls, Pārtha, sheltered in divine nature, and knowing the unchanging source of beings, worship Me with undeviated minds. 13 Ever praising Me and striving with firm

[1] Here *yoga* denotes mystic power.

vows, bowing to Me with devotion, always linked, they honor Me. 14 Yet others, offering with a knowledge-offering, honor Me in oneness, in separateness, and in the multi-form facing everywhere. 15

I am the rite, the offering and the benediction—I alone, the healing herb, the *mantra*, the clarified butter and the oblation. 16 I am the father, mother, creator and grandfather of this world; I am the knowable, the purifier and the sacred vibration *Om*; indeed I am the Ṛg-, Sāma- and Yajur-Veda. 17 I am the way, sustainer, Lord, witness, dwelling and shelter, the kind friend, origin, dissolution, support, receptacle and unperishing seed. 18 It is I who provide warmth and who restrain and release rain. I alone am immortality, O Arjuna—as well as death, being and nonbeing. 19

Those with three sciences,[2] soma-drinkers cleansed of sin, honoring me with offerings, petition passage to heaven. Approaching Surendra's world of merit, they enjoy in heaven the heavenly pleasures of gods. 20 Having enjoyed the vast heavenly world and exhausted their merit, they [again] enter the mortal world. Thus having duly pursued tri-Veda *dharma* and their wished for wishes, they achieve only going and coming. 21

Persons who worship Me thinking of no other, ever diligent—to them I bring support and security. 22 Yet those who devotedly and faithfully offer to other divinities—even *they* offer to Me alone, Kaunteya, irregularly. 23 For I am the only Lord and Enjoyer of all offerings. But they do not recognize Me in truth and so they fall down. 24

Those sworn to gods, go to gods; those sworn to ancestors, go to ancestors; spirit worshippers go to spirits; but My worshipers go to Me. 25 When one dedicates to Me with devotion a leaf, flower, fruit or water, I accept that devoted gift from a

---

[2] "Three sciences" denotes the Ṛg-, Sāma- and Yajur-Veda.

dedicated soul. 26 Whatever you do, whatever you eat, whatever you sacrifice, whatever you gift, whatever trouble you take—make that an offering to Me. 27 Thus you will be freed from good and bad fruits, which are *karma*-bondage. As a liberated soul linked by renunciation-*yoga*, you will come to Me. 28

I am equal to all beings; I neither hate nor favor. But those who honor Me with devotion are in Me, and indeed I am in them. 29 Even if one behaved very badly, if one loves me exclusively, one is to be considered righteous, being rightly resolved. 30 One quickly becomes a *dharma*-soul and enters into lasting peace. O Kaunteya, declare that one devoted to Me is not lost. 31 Indeed, Pārtha, those taking shelter of Me, be they even from bad wombs, or be they women, tradesmen, farmers or workers—they too reach the highest goal. 32 What then of pure *brāhmaṇas*, devotees and royal saints? Thus, having come to this impermanent unhappy world, worship Me! 33 Be mindful of Me, devoted to Me; offer to Me, bow to Me. Thus linking your soul, fully devoted to Me, you will come to Me alone. 34

Chapter 10

The Lord said: Yet again, Mighty-armed, hear My supreme word.
Desiring your good, for you are loved, I shall speak to you. 1
Neither hosts of gods nor great sages know My origin, for I am
wholly the source of gods and great sages. 2 One who knows
Me as unborn and beginningless, the great Lord of worlds, is
unconfused among mortals and is freed from all sins. 3

Reason, knowledge, non-confusion, forgiveness, truth,
discipline, serenity, happiness, unhappiness, becoming, nonexistence, danger and safety, 4 non-harm, equality, satisfaction,
austerity, charity, fame and infamy—these states, in various
forms, arise from Me alone. 5 Seven great ancient sages and
four Manus are born of My mind and share My nature. This
world's progeny comes from them. 6 One who knows in truth
this vast power and *yoga* of Mine engages in unwavering *yoga*.
There is no doubt here. 7

I am the source of all; from Me, all emanates. Realizing
this and filled with feeling, the intelligent devote themselves
to Me. 8 Their thoughts are in Me, their lives rest in Me.
Enlightening one another and always speaking of Me, they find
satisfaction and pleasure. 9 To those that are ever linked and
worship with love, I give the *yoga* of reason by which they come
to Me. 10 For them alone, for mercy's sake, I dispel with the
shining lamp of knowledge the darkness born of ignorance, for
I dwell in the soul's being. 11

Arjuna said: You are the supreme Brahman, supreme
abode and ultimate purifier, the eternal divine Person and original God—unborn and almighty. 12 All seers, such as Devarṣi
Nārada, Asita, Devala and Vyāsa, say this of You, and You in
fact are personally telling me. 13 Keśava, I accept as true all that
You tell me. Neither gods nor demons know Your personality,

Lord. 14 Only You Yourself know Your Self by Your Self, O Supreme Person Who causes beings to be! Lord of beings! God of gods! Master of the world! 15 Kindly describe fully Your vast, divine powers—powers by which You continue to pervade these worlds. 16

O Yogī, how should I understand You while always meditating on You? And in what various states, Lord, am I to meditate on You? 17 Janārdana, recite again at length Your *yoga* and vast power. I am not sated on hearing this nectar. 18

The Lord said: Listen! I shall indeed recite My vast powers, best of Kurus—the main ones, for there is no end to My expansion. 19 I am the Soul, Guḍākeśa, present in every being's heart. In fact, I am the beginning, middle and end of beings. 20 Of Ādityas I am Viṣṇu, among luminaries, the radiant sun. Of Maruts I am Marīci, among lunar mansions, the moon. 21 Of Vedas I am Sāma-veda, of gods I am Vāsava, of senses I am mind, and of beings I am consciousness. 22 Of Rudras I am Śaṅkara, among Yakṣas and Rakṣas, the lord of wealth. Of Vasus I am Fire, I am Meru among towering peaks. 23 Of priests, Pārtha, know Me as Bṛhaspati, the chief. Of military leaders I am Skanda and of water bodies I am the ocean. 24 Of great sages I am Bhṛgu, of words I am the one unperishing syllable. Of sacrifices I am the quiet chant, of stable things, the Himālaya. 25

Of trees I am the holy fig tree; and of god-sages, Nārada. Of Gandharvas I am Citra-ratha and I am sage Kapila among perfected beings. 26 Of horses, know Me as nectar-risen Uccaiḥśravā, of leading elephants, Airāvata, and of human beings, their ruler. 27 Of weapons I am the thunderbolt; among cows, Kāma-dhuk.[1] I am the begetter Kandarpa. Of serpents I am Vāsuki. 28 And I am Ananta among Nāgas. Of great aquatics I am Varuṇa, of ancestors I am Aryamā, and of subduers I am Yama [lord of death]. 29 Of Daityas I am Prahlāda, of impellers

[1] Kāma-dhuk, "Wish-yielder," is a celestial cow that yields all desires.

I am Time, of beasts I am the lion, lord of beasts, and among the winged I am Garuḍa, son of Vinatā. 30 Of purifiers I am purifying wind, of weapon-wielders I am Rāma, of large fish I am the shark; and I am Jāhnavī [the Ganges] among flowing waters. 31

Of creations I am the beginning and end and indeed the middle, Arjuna. Of sciences I am the science of self. Of those stating claims I am the clear conclusion. 32 Of letters I am the letter A, and of compounds I am the pair. I alone am unperishing Time, I the all-facing Creator. 33 I am all-taking death and the coming forth of all that will come. Of the feminine, I am fame, beauty, speech, memory, reason, firmness and forgiveness. 34 So too, of hymns I am the Great Hymn, and of metered chants, the Gāyatrī. Of months I am Trail-head,[2] of seasons, Flower-mine.[3] 35

Of deceivers I am dicing. I am the splendor of the splendid. I am victory. I am resolve. I am the essence of the essential. 36 Of Vṛṣṇis I am Vāsudeva, of Pāṇḍavas, Arjuna. Indeed of sages I am Vyāsa, of thinkers, learned Uśanā. 37 I am the rod among tamers and I am moral conduct among those seeking victory. And, truly, of secrets I am silence. Of the wise I am wisdom. 38 And I am that which is the seed of all beings, Arjuna. No moving or unmoving being can exist without Me. 39

There is no end to my vast divine powers, Scorcher of Foes. Of my vast power's extent I provide *only* an example. 40 Know that each and every being that possesses power, beauty or true excellence springs from a part of My splendor. 41 But then what need have you to learn so much, Arjuna? With a single fragment of Myself, I steadily sustain this entire universe. 42

---

[2] Trailhead: Mārga-śīrṣa (November-December).

[3] Flower-mine: spring.

Chapter 11

Arjuna said: To favor me, You spoke the supreme mystery called *Higher Self*.[1] Those words dispelled my illusion. 1 O Lotus-petal-eyed, I heard from You at length of the becoming and vanishing of beings, and about Your unperishing majesty. 2 Supreme Lord, O Highest Person, I now wish to see Your lordly form as You thus described Yourself! 3 Master, if you think it possible for me to see, then show Me Your unperishing Self, O *Yoga* Lord. 4

The Lord said: Behold, Pārtha, My divine forms by hundreds and thousands, many kinds and colors, in many shapes. 5 Behold Ādityas, Vasus, Rudras, twin Aśvins and Maruts. Behold, Bhārata, many wonders unseen before! 6 Behold now the world entire in one place, in My body, Guḍākeśa, with the moving and unmoving and whatever else you wish to behold! 7 But you are unable to see Me with your eye alone. I give you a divine eye. Behold My ruling *Yoga*! 8

Sañjaya said: Thus speaking, O King, Great *Yoga* Lord Hari then revealed to Pārtha His supreme ruling form: 9 many mouths and eyes, many wondrous visions, many divine ornaments, many divine upraised weapons! 10 It bore raiment, divine garlands, divine scents and ointments, all miraculous, godly, endless—facing everywhere! 11 If a thousand suns could rise at once in the sky, that light might resemble the light of that Great Soul. 12

There, in the body of the God of gods, Pāṇḍava beheld the universe entire in one place, yet variously divided. 13 Filled

[1] The mystery that a Supreme Eternal Person (Kṛṣṇa) is the source of everything.

with wonder, hairs standing up, Dhanañjaya, bowing his head to God [Kṛṣṇa], then spoke: 14

Arjuna said: O God, in Your body I behold Lord Brahmā on the lotus seat, all gods and distinct societies of beings, all sages and divine serpents. 15 On all sides I behold Your infinite form, with many arms, stomachs, faces and eyes. I see no end, nor middle, nor yet beginning of You, Cosmic Lord, Cosmic Form. 16 I behold You with crown, club and disk—a mass of splendor shining everywhere, hard to wholly observe, bright like blazing fire and sun! Immeasurable! 17

You are unperishing, the ultimate knowable. You are the supreme receptacle. You are the unperishing protector of eternal *dharma*. I consider You the eternal Person. 18 I behold You with no beginning, middle or end, of endless prowess and endless arms, with moon and sun Your eyes, and Your mouth a blazing oblation-eating fire as You heat the world with Your splendor. 19 From earth to heaven, You alone pervade this space and all directions. Seeing this Your wondrous fierce form, Great Soul, the three worlds tremble. 20

Indeed these societies of gods enter You; some, fearful, pray with folded hands, saying, "Let us prosper"! Great sages and perfected beings laud You with full ardent praises. 21 Rudras, Ādityas, Vasus, all Sādhyas, Viśvas, Maruts and Heat-drinkers,[2] Gandhavara, Yakṣa, Asura and Siddha groups—all simply gaze at You, amazed! 22 O Great-armed, seeing Your great form with many mouths and eyes, many arms, thighs and feet, many stomachs and many dreadful teeth—the worlds tremble, as do I. 23 Indeed, seeing You touching the sky, blazing with many colors, mouths gaping, immense eyes blazing—my inner self trembles. O Viṣṇu, I find neither peace nor support. 24 Simply seeing Your dreadful teeth and Your faces resembling Time-fire, I do not know the directions. I find no shelter. O Lord of gods, be gracious! O World's Abode! 25

[2] Sages that nourish themselves by "drinking" the steam of hot food.

All these sons of Dhṛta-rāṣṭra, with groups of earthly rulers, Bhīṣma, Droṇa and that Sūta-son, even together with our best fighters, 26 all rushing, enter Your mouths that have dreadful, terrifying teeth. Some [fighters] are clearly seen trapped between teeth with heads pulverized. 27

As rivers' many rapids run to the sea alone, so these mortal-world heroes enter your wildly blazing mouths. 28 As moths, unto destruction, enter blazing fire with full-blown force, so these worlds, unto destruction, enter Your mouths with full-blown force. 29 Fiercely licking all worlds on every side with Your flaming mouths, Viṣṇu, Your rays scorch the universe, filling it with radiance. 30 Declare to me! Who are You, fierce of form? Let me bow to You, most excellent God. Be gracious! I wish to understand You who are the *First*. I do not fathom Your actions. 31

The Lord said: Time I am, World-destroyer, expanded, engaged here to withdraw the worlds. Even without you, all the fighters standing in opposing armies shall not be. 32 Therefore stand up! Gain glory conquering the enemies! Rule a flourishing kingdom! I alone have already slain them; you, Savya-sācī, be but an instrument! 33 Slay those slain by Me: Droṇa, Bhīṣma, Jayadratha, Karṇa and still other battle heroes. Do not waver! Fight! You will conquer the foes in battle. 34

Sañjaya said: Hearing these words of Keśava, diademed Arjuna made a trembling bow with folded hands. Extremely frightened, voice choked, bending forward, he spoke yet again to Kṛṣṇa. 35

Arjuna said: Rightly, Hṛṣīkeśa, the world rejoices at Your glory and grows attached to You. Fearful demons flee in all directions and all accomplished societies bow down. 36 And why should they not bow to You, Great Soul, First Maker—higher yet than Brahmā? O Infinite Lord of gods, Cosmic Abode, You are the unperishing, being and non-being—and what is beyond. 37 Original God, You are the primeval person,

You are the supreme resting place of this universe, the knower, the knowable, the supreme abode. You pervade the universe, O Infinite Form! 38

You are Vāyu, Yama, Agni, Varuṇa, Śaśāṅka, Prajā-pati and the great-grandfather. I bow. Let me bow and bow again to You a thousand times—and again and still more! I bow! I bow to You! 39 I bow in front, then from behind. Let me bow to you from all sides, O All! O Infinite Prowess, Unmeasured Force. You encompass all, and thus *You are all.* 40

Thinking You a *friend*, I imposed myself, not knowing this Your glory. Out of madness or love, I said "O Kṛṣṇa, Yādava, friend"! Just to tease, I insulted You, Acyuta, in sporting, resting, sitting and eating—alone or even in company. Thus I beg You, the immeasurable, to forgive me. 41–42

You are the Father of the moving and unmoving world, and You are the world's venerable Teacher above teachers. You have no equal—whence one superior? Unmatched is Your power, even in [all] three worlds. 43 Therefore, bowing, prostrating my body, I beg You, worshipful Lord, be kind to me. Like father to son, friend to friend, lover to lover, O God, be lenient with me! 44

Seeing what was never seen, I am thrilled and my mind is shaken with fear. Be kind, Lord of gods, World's Dwelling. Show to me only *that* form of God. 45 I wish to see You just so: with crown and club, disc in hand. O Thousand-armed, O Cosmic Form, appear in just that four-armed form. 46

The Lord said: Being pleased with you Arjuna, from My Self-*yoga* I revealed this exceptional primeval form, made of splendor, universal, infinite, unseen before by any other. 47 Not by Vedas, sacrifices or studies, not by gifts nor rites nor harsh penances can any but you in the human realm see Me in such a form, Kuru-hero. 48 Be not alarmed or bewildered on seeing such a frightful form of Mine. Fear dispelled, mind joyful, behold again *this* form of Mine alone! 49

Sañjaya said: Thus speaking to Arjuna and calming that fearful one, the Great Soul Vāsudeva revealed His very own form, assuming again a sublime, beautiful body. 50

Arjuna said: Janārdana, seeing this, Your sublime human-like form I am now restored, rational, natural. 51

The Lord said: The form of Mine that you have just beheld is very hard to see. Even gods ever yearn for a vision of this form. 52 Not by Vedas, nor austerity, nor giving, nor sacrifice can I be seen as you saw Me. 53 But by exclusive devotion, Arjuna, it is possible to know and see Me in truth, and to attain Me, O Scorcher of Foes. 54 One who enacts actions for Me, taking Me as supreme, who is devoted to Me and devoid of attachment, and who does not hate any being—that person comes to Me, Pāṇḍava. 55

Chapter 12

Arjuna said: The devotees thus worship You, always linked,
while others worship the unperishing Invisible. Which of these
know *yoga* best? 1

The Lord said: Those who worship Me with transcendent faith, ever linked, fixing their mind in Me, I regard as
most linked in *yoga*. 2 But those who worship the unperishing, ineffable Invisible that exists everywhere, inconceivable,
unchanging, unmoving and fixed, 3 who control the set of
senses, judging fairly everywhere, intent on every being's
good—they achieve Me alone. 4

Those with minds attached to the Invisible take far greater
trouble. With difficulty, the embodied make the invisible passage. 5 But those releasing all actions to Me, devoted to Me,
who worship Me by meditating with pure exclusive *yoga*, 6
their minds fixed in Me—they I uplift without delay from the
death-cycle ocean, O Pārtha. 7

Fix your mind in Me alone, invest your reason in Me;
you shall henceforth dwell in Me alone, no doubt. 8 If you are
unable to fully focus your mind steadily in Me, then seek to
attain Me by practicing *yoga*, Dhanañjaya. 9 If you are not even
able to practice, be devoted to My work; working for My sake,
you will surely attain perfection. 10 If this too you are unable
to do, then, sheltered in My *yoga* and self-possessed, give up all
action-fruits. 11

Knowledge is better than practice. Meditation surpasses
knowledge. Letting go of action-fruit is better than meditation.
Peace comes at once from letting go. 12

Not hating any being, friendly and also kind, with no *I* and *mine*, equal in sorrow and joy, forgiving, 13 an ever-satisfied *yogī*, self-restrained, of firm conviction, investing mind and intelligence in Me—one so devoted to Me is dear to Me. 14 One who does not distress the world and who the world does not distress, who is free from exulting, intolerance, fear and affliction—that one too is dear to Me. 15

Impartial, decent, expert, neutral, unperplexed, letting go in all undertakings—one so devoted to Me is dear to Me. 16 One who neither exults nor hates nor grieves nor yearns—a devoted soul who lets go in weal and woe—that one is dear to Me. 17 Equal to foe and friend, to honor and dishonor, equal in cold, heat, joy and sorrow, devoid of attachment, 18 equal in slander and praise, silent, satisfied with whatever, without home, of steady mind—that devoted person is dear to Me. 19 Truly those who revere this immortal *dharma* as spoken, trusting it, dedicated to Me—those devotees are exceedingly dear to Me. 20

Chapter 13

Arjuna said: Keśava, I want to understand nature and soul, field and field-knower, knowledge and the knowable. 1

The Lord said: This body, Kaunteya, is termed the *field*. Its knowers call one who understands it a *field-knower*. 2 Understand Me also as field-knower in all fields, Bhārata. I consider knowledge to be this knowledge of field and field-knower. 3

Now briefly hear from Me what this field is—its nature, transformations and source—and who empowers it. 4 This is severally sung by seers, variously with diverse hymns, and indeed by *Brahma-sūtra*'s rational, conclusive words. 5

The gross elements, egotism, reason, the unmanifest, eleven senses[1] and five sense-objects, 6 desire, hatred, joy, sorrow, the amalgam, awareness and will—this, in summary, is termed the field with transformations. 7

Pridelessness, non-duplicity, not harming, forgiveness, rectitude, serving spiritual guides, cleanliness, steadiness, self-control, 8 dispassion for sense objects, non-egotism, reflecting on the painful flaws of birth, death, old age and disease, 9 detachment, not obsessing over children, spouse, home, etc., constant equal-mindedness in desired and undesired occurrences, 10 unswerving devotion to Me through exclusive *yoga*, resorting to a secluded place, not delighting in public meetings, 11 constancy in self-knowledge, and seeing the value of

[1] Eleven senses: sight, hearing, smell, taste and touch; arms, legs, speech, reproductive organ and anus; the mind.

knowing truth—this is declared to be knowledge. What is otherwise is ignorance. 12

I shall declare to you the knowable, knowing which one enjoys the immortal: beginningless Brahman, subordinate to Me, and said to be neither being nor nonbeing. 13 Everywhere are its hands and feet, everywhere its eyes, head and mouth. It hears everywhere in this world. Encompassing all, it stands. 14

Resembling all sense modes, it is devoid of all senses; unattached, it alone sustains all—modeless and mode-ruler. 15 Outside and inside of beings, unmoving and yet moving, it is too subtle to grasp, far away and near. 16 Undivided in beings, it stands as if divided. Sustainer of beings, it is to be known as swallower and producer. 17 Of lights, it is that light beyond darkness. It is knowledge, knowable and knowledge-goal—present in everyone's heart. 18

Thus field, knowledge and knowable are briefly described. Understanding this, My devotee reaches My state of being. 19

Know that nature and soul are actually both beginningless. Know too that transformations and modes arise from nature. 20 Nature is said to be the reason for cause, effect and agency. Soul is said to be the reason for the experience of joy and sorrow. 21 Indeed, present in nature, soul experiences nature-born modes. Clinging to modes causes soul's birth in good and bad wombs. 22

Witness, Permitter, Sustainer, Enjoyer, Great Lord—He indeed is said to be the Supreme Self in this body, the Highest Person. 23 One who thus knows soul and nature, with modes, does not take birth again, however living at present. 24

Some see self in Self by self through meditation, others through analysis-*yoga*, and others by action-*yoga*. 25 Still others, not thus knowing, approach upon hearing from others. Dedicated to hearing, even they do truly cross over death. 26

Know that any entity at all, fixed or moving, takes birth when field and field-knower connect. 27

One *sees*, who sees the Supreme Lord standing equally in all beings, unperishing as they perish. 28 In fact, seeing the Lord abiding equally everywhere, one does not harm self by self. Then one travels on the highest path. 29

Actions are being fully done by nature alone. One *sees*, who thus sees self as non-doer. 30 When one perceives that [all] beings' distinct states stand in One and expand from That alone, one then advances to *Brahman*. 31 Beginningless, modeless, this unchanging Supreme Soul does not decline. Though present in the body, He neither acts nor is tainted. 32 Just as all-pervading space, due to its subtlety, is not sullied, so the self that pervades the body is not sullied. 33 Just as one sun illumines all this world, so the one in the field illumines the whole field, Bhārata. 34 They reach the Supreme who thus know with knowledge-eye the difference between field and field-knower and the liberation of beings from nature. 35

Chapter 14

The Lord said: Once more I shall declare the ultimate knowledge of all knowledge, knowing which all sages went from here
to the supreme perfection. 1 Relying on this knowledge, they
came to share My nature. Even at creation, they do not take
birth; and at dissolution, they are not perplexed. 2

My womb is the Great Brahman.[1] In it I place the embryo.
Thus comes the coming to be of all beings, Bhārata. 3 Whatever
forms come to be in all wombs, Kaunteya, Great Brahman is
their womb, I their seed-giving Father. 4

Goodness, passion, darkness—modes born of nature—
bind the unchanging embodied in the body, O Great-armed. 5
Among them, goodness, being unsullied, gives light and is free
of malady. It binds by attachment to joy and knowledge, O
sinless one. 6 Know that craving, arising from attachment
and desire, is the very self of passion. It binds the embodied,
Kaunteya, by attachment to action. 7 Know that darkness, born
of ignorance, bewilders all embodied beings. It binds by madness, sloth and sleep. 8

Know that goodness prevails in joy, Bhārata, and passion
in action, whereas darkness, covering knowledge, prevails
in madness. 9 Overcoming passion and darkness, goodness
comes forth, Bhārata; so too does passion overcome goodness
and darkness, and darkness overcome goodness and passion. 10

---

[1] The Great, Brahman: The Great, *mahat*, refers to the *mahat-tattva*, the *great principle*, the total material energy, which the Lord impregnates with the aggregate of *karma*-weighted souls. This *mahat*, total material energy, is Kṛṣṇa's energy, as He explains at 7.4, and is thus also ultimately Brahman.

When clarity occurs in all this body's gates, when there is knowledge, then know that goodness prospers. 11 Greed, striving, enterprise, stress, longing—these appear when passion prospers, Best of Bharatas. 12 No clarity, no striving, only madness and illusion—these [symptoms] appear when darkness prospers, Kuru-son. 13

Meeting death while goodness prospers, the embodied attains to spotless worlds of highest knowers. 14 Meeting death while passion prospers, one is born among those who cling to action. And so, dying in darkness, one is born from wombs of fools. 15

They say that righteous action's fruit is good and unsullied, while passion's fruit is sorrow, and darkness' fruit is ignorance. 16 Knowledge arises from goodness, and greed alone, from passion. Madness and delusion come from darkness, as does ignorance. 17

Upward go those in goodness, while those in passion stay in the middle, and those living in the lowest quality, darkness, go down. 18 A seer who perceives no other doer but modes, and sees what is above modes, attains My state of being. 19 Going beyond these three modes, which arise from the body, the embodied is freed from birth, death and old age miseries and enjoys the immortal. 20

Arjuna said: By what symptoms has one gone beyond these three modes, Master? What is one's conduct? And how does one transcend these three modes? 21

The Lord said: One who does not hate clarity, striving or even illusion when they surge, Pāṇḍava, or miss them when they cease, 22 who is seated as if seated apart, not deviated by modes, who thinks "*the modes are acting*," standing firm without wavering, 23 who is self-situated, steadfast, equal towards sorrow and joy, soil, stone and gold, pleasing and displeasing events, censure and praise of self, 24 who is equal in honor and dishonor, equal to friends and enemies, a renouncer in all endeavors—that one is said to have gone beyond the modes. 25

And one who serves Me with undeviating *bhakti-yoga* goes fully beyond these modes and qualifies for Brahman existence. 26 Indeed I am the foundation of immortal, unperishing Brahman, of everlasting *dharma* and of absolute joy. 27

Chapter 15

The Lord said: They tell of an unperishing banyan tree with
roots up and branches down. Its leaves are Vedic hymns. One
who knows it, knows the Veda. 1 Its branches extend down
and up, thriving on modes. Sense-objects are its new shoots;
and its roots, bound to actions, spread down far and wide in
the human world. 2

Its true form is not perceived here, nor its end, beginning and foundation. Cutting down, with the firm weapon of
detachment, this deeply rooted banyan, 3 one must then search
for that place, reaching which they never return, [resolving]: "I
submit to Him alone, the First Person from Whom the ancient
origin proceeded." 4

Free of conceit and confusion, the attachment flaw
defeated, ever fixed on Higher Self, withdrawn from desires,
delivered from dualities named joy and sorrow—the unconfused go to that unperishing place. 5 Sun does not light it,
nor moon, nor fire. Going there, they never return. That is My
supreme abode. 6

In the living world, the eternal living being, part of Me
alone, presides over matter-based senses, whose sixth[1] is
mind. 7 This master acquires and quits a body, and taking
these [senses], wanders like wind taking scents from a source. 8
Standing over sight, hearing, touch, taste, smell and mind, he
visits sense objects. 9 The confused do not perceive him passing away, or indeed staying [in the body], or enjoying, joined
to modes. Those with eyes of knowledge see. 10 Striving *yogīs*

[1] Senses whose sixth is mind: mind is considered to be a sixth sense that coordinates the other five.

see him abiding in Self. The undutiful and unmindful, though
striving, do not see this.[2] 11

The splendor in the sun that lights up the whole world,
and that in moon and fire—know it to be My own splendor. 12
Entering Earth, I preserve beings with vigor; becoming the
nectar-made moon, I nourish all plants. 13 Becoming the diges-
tive fire abiding in bodies of breathing beings, I mingle with
in- and out-breath and digest four-fold food.[3] 14 I dwell deep in
the heart of all. From me come memory, knowledge and forgetting. By all Vedas, I alone am to be known. I made Vedānta and
I alone know the Veda. 15

These two persons exist in the world: the perishing and
the truly unperishing. Perishing are all beings; the unperishing
one is said to stand at the peak. 16 But the Ultimate Person is
another called the Supreme Soul. He is the unchanging Lord—
who, entering them, sustains the three worlds. 17

Because I am supreme, beyond the perishing and even the
unperishing, I am thus celebrated in the world and the Veda
as the Ultimate Person. 18 The unbewildered who thus know
Me as the Ultimate Person, know all and devote themselves to
Me with all their being, Bhārata. 19 Sinless one, I have thus
told you most confidential scripture. Learning this, one must
be learned, with duty done, Bhārata. 20

[2] The English translation of verses 9, 10 and 11 reflect the fact that the Sanskrit of these verses happens to contain the *masculine* pronouns "he" and "him."

[3] Four-fold food: foods that are either swallowed, chewed, licked or sucked.

Chapter 16

Fearlessness, purity of being, perseverance in knowledge-
yoga, generosity, discipline, sacrifice, sacred study, austerity,
honesty, 1 non-harm, truth, non-anger, letting go, peace, non-
slander, kindness to living beings, non-greed, gentleness,
modesty, non-caprice, 2 energy, forgiveness, resolve, cleanliness, non-aggression, non-arrogance—these exist in one born
to godly assets. 3

One born to ungodly assets possesses deceit, conceit, malice, anger, harshness and ignorance. 4 It is understood that
godly assets lead to freedom, the ungodly to bondage. Do not
worry, Pāṇḍava, you are born to godly assets. 5

Beings have but two natures in this world: godly and
ungodly. The godly has been extensively taught. Pārtha, hear
from Me of the ungodly. 6

Ungodly people know neither what nor what not to do.
Neither cleanliness nor good conduct nor truth exists in
them. 7 They claim the world has no truth, no foundation, no
Lord—that it arose from interaction and is based on nothing
but selfish motives. 8 Standing firm on this view, these lost
malign souls of little reason and savage deeds come forth to
destroy the world. 9 Hypocrites full of pride and presumption,
they cling to insatiable desire. They proceed in delusion, con-
ceiving unreal conceptions, sworn to the unclean. 10 Resigned
until death to immeasurable anxiety, they are convinced that
desire-gratification is supreme. 11 Bound by hundreds of
desire-chains, filled with lust and anger, they strive unjustly to
collect wealth for selfish pleasure. 12

"I attained this longing today; I *shall* achieve that one. This wealth is mine; this other wealth *will* be mine. 13 I killed that enemy; I will kill others still. I am lord! I am the enjoyer! I am perfect, powerful, happy! 14 I am rich, of noble descent. Who else is like me? I shall sacrifice, give charity and make merry." Thus ignorance bewilders them. 15

Meandering in many mental states, wrapped in illusion's net, clinging to desire gratification, they fall into an unclean hell. 16 Fully self-esteemed, stubborn, filled with pride and presumption over wealth, they hypocritically offer with offerings in name, with no regard for rules. 17 Hating Me in their own and others' bodies, the enviers fully rely on egotism, strength, insolence, will and rage. 18 I perpetually throw these hating, cruel, lowest of men into transmigrations in truly demonic wombs. 19 Falling into a demonic womb in birth after birth, surely not achieving Me, such fools go to the lowest state. 20

Threefold is this soul-ruining gateway to hell: lust, anger and greed. Therefore one should give up these three. 21 Freed of these three gateways to darkness, one does great good for the soul and then goes to the highest state. 22

Avoiding scripture's rule, one who lives by acting on desires reaches neither perfection nor happiness nor the highest state. 23 Therefore, in determining duty and non-duty, scripture is your measure. Knowing scripture's stated rule, you ought to do your duty here. 24

Chapter 17

Arjuna said: What is the status of those who faithfully sacrifice but avoid scripture's rule? Is it goodness, passion or darkness? 1

The Lord said: The embodied soul's faith, born of one's nature, is of three kinds: good, passionate and dark. Hear about this. 2 Everyone has faith, Bhārata, according to their nature. A person is made of faith. One becomes just what one believes. 3

Those in goodness, sacrifice to gods, those in passion, to spirits and guardians.[1] Other people, in darkness, sacrifice to the departed and to troops of ghosts. 4 Filled with desire and passion, people joined to deceit and egoism undergo horrible austerity, 5 mindlessly plaguing the body's elements—*and Me as well, present in the body.* Know these people to be of ungodly resolve. 6

Now even food is dear to everyone in three ways, so too offering, austerity and charity. Hear of these divisions. 7

Those in goodness enjoy foods that increase longevity, energy, strength, health, joy and contentment, and that are tasty, appealing, lasting and hearty. 8 Foods dear to the passionate are bitter, sour, salty, too hot, pungent and burning; they produce pain, affliction and disease. 9 Those in darkness like food that is spoiled, flavorless, putrid and stale—and even impure leftovers. 10

---

[1] Spirits and guardians indicates yakṣas and rakṣas, which may also refer to specific groups of ethereal and, at times, dangerous beings.

An offering in goodness, fixed by precept, is offered with full concentration by those not seeking fruits, the mind simply thinking, “it is right to offer.” 11 But know that a passionate offering is offered hypocritically, seeking the fruit, O Best of Bhāratas. 12 They deem as dark an offering bereft of precept, with no sharing of food, bereft of *mantra*, with no gifts to priests, and stripped of faith. 13

Honor to gods, gurus, the twice-born and the wise, cleanliness, rectitude, chastity and doing no harm—these are said to comprise bodily austerity. 14 True, pleasing, beneficial speech that does not disturb as well as regular study of scripture—these are said to comprise speech austerity. 15 Serenity of mind, gentleness, quietude, self-control and purity of being—these are said to comprise mental austerity. 16

They deem to be in goodness the threefold austerity endured with highest faith by linked people not seeking fruits. 17 Erratic impermanent austerity, done hypocritically for respect, prestige and honor, is deemed to be in passion. 18 Austerity done with foolish obstinacy and self-harm, or to destroy an enemy, is declared to be in darkness. 19

Thinking, “it is right to give,” a gift given to one not serving the giver, at the right place and time, to the right recipient, is held to be in goodness. 20 A gift given grudgingly to gain service in return—or, again, aiming at the fruit—is held to be in passion. 21 A disrespectful, insulting gift, given at the wrong place and time to the wrong recipient, is declared to be in darkness. 22

Om tat sat is held to be a threefold indication of Brahman; by it, *brāhmaṇas*, Vedas and offerings were ordained of old. 23 Therefore, with the uttering of *Om*, authorized acts of sacrifice, charity and austerity ever proceed among Brahman-speakers; 24 and with *Tad*, those seeking liberation, not aiming at fruits, enact acts of sacrifice, austerity and various acts of charity. 25 *Sat* is recited in true and righteous being, and is also thus used in commended action, Pārtha. 26 Steadiness in sacrifice, austerity and charity are said to constitute *Sat*; and action for that purpose is thus called *Sat*. 27 Without faith, whatever is offered, given and done as austerity or good deed is called non-*Sat*, Pārtha, and is not *Tad*[2]—neither here nor in the hereafter. 28

[2] *Tad* is literally the neuter demonstrative pronoun *That*, and thus stands for a real truth or object that can be demonstrated and known. Thus apparently pious actions performed without faith are not the real thing itself—i.e., not the real *that*.

Chapter 18

Arjuna said: O Great-armed slayer of Keśi, O Hṛṣīkeśa, I wish to know, separately, the truth about renouncing and letting go. 1

The Lord said: The wise know renouncing as putting aside selfish actions; the clear-sighted call letting go the letting go of all action-fruits. 2 Some sages claim that action is flawed and to be let go; others claim that acts of sacrifice, charity and austerity are not to be let go. 3 Hear my conclusion about letting go, Best of Bharatas. Three ways of letting go are described, O Man-tiger. 4 One must not let go of sacrifice, charity and austerity; these are to be done. Sacrifice, charity and austerity purify even sages. 5 Thus one should indeed perform these actions, letting go of attachment and fruits. This is my certain and final view, Pārtha. 6

Renouncing prescribed action is not right; letting it go due to confusion is declared to be in darkness. 7 One who would let go of duty, fearing bodily discomfort, thinking it "miserable," has merely let go in passion and cannot gain the fruit of letting go. 8 When one does prescribed duty, Arjuna, thinking only, "it is to be done," and abandons attachment and fruit—that letting go is deemed in goodness. 9

An intelligent renouncer, filled with goodness, with doubts dispelled, neither hates inconvenient duty nor clings to the convenient. 10 One who bears a body cannot possibly let go of actions entirely. Yet one who lets go of action's fruits is said to be one who has let go. 11 Action's threefold fruit—desired, undesired and mixed—comes to those who do not let go, but never to renouncers. 12

O Great-armed, learn from Me, as taught in conclu-
sive *Sāṅkhya*,[1] these five causes for success in all actions: 13
place, doer, diverse means, diverse efforts—and, of course,
Providence. 14 Whatever right or wrong action a person undertakes with body, mind and speech, these five are the causes. 15
This being so, a dull-witted person of unformed reason, who
sees self alone as doer, does not see. 16 One whose nature is not
ego-centered, whose reason is not tainted, does not kill, even
when killing these people, and is not bound. 17

Knowledge, knowable and knower are the threefold
action-impetus. Means, action and doer are the threefold sum
of action. 18 In mode-analysis, knowledge, action and doer are
stated to be threefold by mode-divisions. Duly hear of these as
well. 19

Learn that knowledge in goodness is that by which one
sees a single unchanging reality in all beings, undivided in the
divided. 20 Learn that knowledge in passion is that by which
one sees separately in all beings various natures of separate
types. 21 But knowledge that clings irrationally to one task as
all, that is meager and lacks a sense of truth, is declared to be
in darkness. 22

Prescribed action, free of attachment, done without passion or aversion by one not seeking the fruit, is said to be in
goodness. 23 But action done by one seeking selfish pleasure,
or done with egotism and much trouble, is declared to be in
passion. 24 Action undertaken in illusion, disregarding consequences, waste, harm and human limits, is said to be in
darkness. 25

Free of attachment and self-promotion, filled with determination and resolve, unchanging in success and failure, a doer
is said to be in goodness. 26 Attached, seeking action's fruit,
greedy, violent, unclean, filled with thrills and misery, a doer

---

[1] *Sāṅkhya*: an ancient philosophical system that enumerates fundamental entities and describes their relationships.

is said to be in passion. 27 Unfit, vulgar, stubborn, depraved, malicious, morose and procrastinating, a doer is said to be in darkness. 28

Hear, Dhanañjaya, of the threefold modal division of reason and resolve, fully and severally stated. 29 Reason in goodness understands engagement and disengagement, duty and non-duty, danger and non-danger, bondage and freedom, Pārtha. 30 By reason in passion one imprecisely understands *dharma* and non-*dharma*, duty and non-duty, Pārtha. 31 Covered by darkness, reason that thinks non-*dharma* is *dharma*, and takes all matters backwards, Pārtha, is reason in darkness. 32

Resolve by which mind, life, senses and duty are sustained with undeviating *yoga*, is resolve in goodness, Pārtha. 33 Resolve that is eager for fruits, that sustains *dharma*, desire and interest with attachment, is resolve in passion, Pārtha. 34 And dim-witted resolve that does not let go of sleep, fear, lamentation, depression and even madness, is resolve in darkness, Pārtha. 35

But now hear from Me, Best of Bharatas, of the threefold happiness one enjoys by practice, reaching sorrow's end. 36 That which is like poison at first and resembles nectar at last is said to be happiness in goodness, born of clarity and self-understanding. 37 Happiness from the contact of senses with their objects resembles nectar at first and poison at last, and is held to be in passion. 38 Happiness that deludes the soul at the start and in the outcome, arising from sleep, sloth and madness, is declared to be in ignorance. 39

There is no being on earth, nor yet among gods in heaven, who is free of these three nature-born modes. 40 For *brāhmaṇas, kṣatriyas, vaiśyas* and *śūdras*,[2] Scorcher of Foes, their nature-born modes divide their duties. 41

---

[2] *Brāhmaṇas*: teachers and priests; *kṣatriyas*: rulers and warriors; *vaiśyas*: landowners and tradesmen; *śūdras*: workers and artisans.

Calmness, purity, discipline, austerity and forbearance as well as rectitude, knowledge, wisdom and faith in God are a *brāhmaṇa's* work, born of one's nature. 42 Heroism, power, resolve and skill as well as charity, a ruling nature and not fleeing a fight are a *kṣatriya's* work, born of one's nature. 43 Farming, cow protection and trade are a *vaiśya's* work, born of one's nature; and a *śudra*'s work, born of one's nature, lies in assisting. 44 Each person, dedicated to one's own work, achieves full perfection. Hear how one finds perfection engaged in one's own work. 45

He from Whom beings emanate and by Whom all this is pervaded—worshipping Him by one's duty, a human being finds perfection. 46 Better is one's own *dharma* imperfect than another's *dharma* well performed. Doing duty set by one's nature, one incurs no offense. 47 One should not give up innate work, even if flawed. Flaws surely cover all undertakings as smoke covers fire. 48

Self-controlled, with reason everywhere detached and longings dispersed, one achieves by renunciation the supreme perfection of freedom from *karma*. 49 Learn from Me in simple synopsis how just as one achieves perfection so one attains Brahman, the highest status of knowledge. 50 Linked by pure reason, resolutely restraining self, giving up sense objects like sound, casting off passion and aversion, 51 seeking seclusion, eating little, with speech, body and mind controlled, ever focused on meditation-*yoga*, braced by dispassion, 52 letting go of egotism, power, pride, lust, anger and property, peaceful, with no "*mine*"—one qualifies for Brahman existence. 53

Living in Brahman, a serene soul does not grieve or yearn—and, equal to all beings, attains highest devotion to Me. 54 By devotion, one recognizes Me, My extent, and what I am in truth. Knowing Me in truth, one thereupon returns to Me. 55 Though always performing all actions, at My shelter and by My grace one achieves the eternal, unperishing position. 56

By awareness, relinquishing all actions to Me and dedicated to Me, relying on the *yoga* of reason, be ever mindful of Me. 57 Mindful of Me, by My grace, you will pass over all obstacles. But if from egotism you will not hear, you will be lost. 58 Relying on egotism, if you think, "I shall not fight," that decision is wrong. Nature will impel you. 59 Kaunteya, you are bound by *your* work born of *your* nature. That which, from illusion, you do not wish to do, you will do even against your wish. 60

The Lord of all beings resides in the region of the heart, Arjuna, making all beings wander as they ride in illusion on the [bodily] machine. 61 Go to Him alone for shelter with all your being, Bhārata. By His grace you shall attain supreme peace, the everlasting abode. 62

Thus I have taught you knowledge more secret than the secret. Reflecting on this fully, do as you wish. 63 Once more, hear My supreme word, the most secret of all. You are very well loved by Me, so I shall speak for your good. 64 Be mindful of Me and devoted to Me, offer to Me, bow to Me. You will come to Me alone. I promise you this truly, for I love you. 65 Giving up all *dharmas*, come to Me alone for shelter. I shall free you from all evils, do not worry. 66

This is never to be spoken to the undisciplined, the non-devout, to one not wishing to hear nor to one who envies Me. 67 One who will explain this supreme secret among My devotees renders the highest devotion to Me and will come to Me alone without doubt. 68 No other among human beings is most dear to Me, nor will there be any other on earth more dear than that person. 69 And I deem it that one who studies this dharmic dialogue of ours worships Me by the offering of reason. 70 And a faithful, non-envious person who can listen—that one too is freed and can attain the prospering worlds for those of pious deeds. 71

Did you hear this, Pārtha, with one-pointed mind? Has your confusion caused by ignorance vanished, Dhanañjaya? 72

Arjuna said: By Your Grace, Acyuta, illusion is gone, memory regained. I stand firm, free of doubt. I shall execute Your word. 73

Sañjaya said: Thus I heard this wonderful, hair-raising dialogue of Vāsudeva and great soul Pārtha. 74 By Vyāsa's grace, I heard this supreme mystery of *yoga*, personally spoken by *Yoga*-Lord Kṛṣṇa Himself. 75 O King! Remembering! Remembering this wondrous dialogue of Keśava and Arjuna, I incessantly rejoice! 76 And remembering *that!* Remembering Hari's most amazing form, great is my wonder, O King! And I rejoice again and again! 77 Where there is *Yoga*-Lord Kṛṣṇa, where there is bow-wielding Pārtha, *there* is fortune, victory, power and fixed right conduct. Thus I conclude. 7

Bibliography

Bhaktivedanta Swami Prabhupāda, A.C., trans. and comm. *Bhagavad-gītā As It Is*. 2nd ed. Los Angeles: Bhaktivedanta Book Trust, 1989.

MacDonell, Arthur Anthony. *A Sanskrit Grammar for Students*. London: Oxford University Press, 1927.

Monier-Williams, Monier. *A Sanskrit-English Dictionary*. Oxford Clarendon Press, [1899] 1974.

Radhakrishnan, S., trans. and comm. *The Bhagavadgītā*. 1st ed. New York: Harper & Row, 1973.

Schweig, Graham M. *Bhagavad-gītā: The Beloved Lord's Secret Love Song*. New York: HarperOne, 2007.

Index to Comprehensive Guide

NOTE: Kṛṣṇa is not covered extensively in this index because He appears throughout the entirety of the *Comprehensive Guide*. As such, the *Guide's* Table of Contents itself is a reliable index to topics regarding Kṛṣṇa.

Y

Acknowledgments[1]

With deep gratitude, I acknowledge and thank those whose invaluable help made this book possible. I give here a partial list, with sincere apologies to those who may have been overlooked.

I first thank my spiritual master, Śrīla Prabhupāda, without whom I would know virtually nothing of the *Bhagavad-gītā*, nor of myself. His is the merit in this work, mine the deficiencies. I thank and esteem all his predecessor teachers, who preserved the sacred text through long centuries.

My thanks must go to Ali Krishna (Alysia Radder), who brilliantly and lovingly helped to found and develop our media team; Brahmatirtha (Bob Cohen), my alter ego, who rendered valuable help to this and every other project of mine; Aja (Allan Andersson), my dear spiritual brother, who lent his expert hand to the editing and production; my spiritual sister and old friend Mayapriya (Candace Long), who designed and formatted the book; Duhkha-hantri (Donna DeAngelis), an old friend and spiritual sister who did copy-editing, and who rendered invaluable help with all my previous books; Krishna Kshetra Swami (Kenneth Valpey), a dear spiritual brother and gifted scholar, who reviewed the translation; Giridhari (Gustavo Dauster), my dear disciple who always helps with everything; Advaita Candra (Alister Taylor), my old friend and walking partner, whose publishing house has gone out of its way to work with

[1] For personal Sanskrit names of the production staff, including the author, we chose to use the non-academic spelling that is familiar to most people.

us on this book; and Danesha (Daniel Laflor) who designed the cover.

My thanks also to my mentor at Sanskrit Harvard, Dr. Michael Witzel, and to the Harvard "experience," which helped me to translate not only for an insider audience, but for a general audience as well.

Finally I offer my heartfelt gratitude to my dear and departed parents, whose unstinting love and generosity made possible more things than I can recount; and I thank my brothers Allen and Robert for their generosity and support.